FOR THE LOVE
OF GOD

FOR THE
LOVE OF GOD

The Faith and Future of the American Nun

LUCY KAYLIN

William Morrow
An Imprint of HarperCollins*Publishers*

HarperCollins books may be purchased for educational, business, or sales promotional use. For information please write: Special Markets Department, HarperCollins Publishers Inc., 10 East 53rd Street, New York, NY 10022.

FIRST EDITION

Designed by Bernard Klein

Printed on acid-free paper

Library of Congress Cataloging-in-Publication Data

Kaylin, Lucy.
    For the love of God : the faith and future of the American nun / Lucy Kaylin.—1st ed.
        p. cm.
    ISBN 0-688-15458-1
    1. Nuns—United States—History—20th century.   2. Monasticism and religious orders for women—United States—History—20th century.   3. Monastic and religious life of women—United States—History—20th century.   4. Catholic Church—United States—History—20th century.   5. United States—Church history. 6. Vatican Council (2nd : 1962–1965)   I. Title.
    BX4220.U6 K39 2000
    271'.90073'0904—dc21   00–039439

00 01 02 03 04 RRD 10 9 8 7 6 5 4 3 2 1

For Sophie

CONTENTS

ACKNOWLEDGMENTS

Four years ago, I began calling nuns out of the blue and essentially asking them to tell all—about their intense commitment to a mysterious way of life and the sacrifices that life entails. I will never get over the generosity with which these women greeted my request. Some invited me in, fed me, and gave me a place to stay; all shared freely of their time and insights. Without naming them here, I extend my heartfelt thanks to every woman represented in these pages.

Along the way I received much assistance from many quarters. For their contributions, I am indebted to: Jeannette Batz; Anne Bergeron; Carol Bogart; Cynthia Cathcart; Andrew Cooperman; Barbara Delaney; Mother Marie Edward Deutsch, OP; Fr. James Empereur, SJ; David Granger; Janet Harrison; the Reverend Deane P. Higgs; Sr. Pat Kenoyer, SL; Sr. Genevieve Keusenkothen, DC; the Kirk family of Cuero, TX; Frances Kissling; Dennis Krausnick; Thomas R. Martin, Ph.D.; Terry McDevitt; Thomas F. X. Noble, Ph.D.; Hyacinth Pottinger; Sr. Joseph Powers, OP; Sr. Catherine Quinn, PBVM; Sr. Deanna Sabetta, CND; Sr. Cathy Smith, SL; Margaret Susan Thompson and everyone on Sister-L; Sr. Ann Patrick Ware, SL; and Bo Young.

For their patience and interest I thank my colleagues at *GQ* magazine, and most of all Art Cooper, the editor-in-chief. Although Art may seem an unlikely patron of nun-related endeavors, he made the writing of this book possible—in countless ways.

For their savvy guidance and fierce support I am more grateful than I could possibly say to my agents Bill Clegg and Kathy Robbins. Among other things they led me to Doris Cooper, formerly of William Morrow, whose early and passionate enthusiasm shaped this book. Without missing a beat, Morrow senior editor Meaghan Dowling picked up where Doris left off, shepherding the project to completion with skill and care. I am grateful to both editors, as well as to Meaghan's assistant, Kelli Martin.

A million thanks for the considerable contributions of my astute readers: Lisa Henricksson; Jennifer Kaylin; Sr. Marie-Celine Miranda, OSU; and Elizabeth M. Welch. For her dogged fact-checking and extensive input I am indebted to Mary Flick. Thanks also to the great Jo Ann McNamara for those extraordinarily nourishing lunches.

Thanks is a meager word for what I owe my parents, Peggy and Walter Kaylin; anything of value that I have managed to achieve is a result of their total faith in me.

Finally, my unending gratitude goes to Kimball Higgs for seeing me through with his customary grace and unquestioning love. For her ineffable role in all of this I thank Sophie Kaylin Higgs, my daily proof of miracles.

INTRODUCTION

BEFORE I BEGAN THE RESEARCH for this book, I had never once met or spoken with a nun. I viewed this as an asset. Having grown up without religion, I felt sure that I was free of preconceived notions. As it turned out, I was in for a few surprises.

The first came during my visit to the Sisters of Loretto at the Foot of the Cross, a Catholic community almost two centuries old. With its dormlike buildings and vast, verdant acreage, the Loretto motherhouse in central Kentucky has the feel of a college campus during summer break. That is, until you notice the neatly coifed septuagenarians strolling around in sensible clothes, as well as the number of small stairways that have been smoothed over with cement in the interest of wheelchair accessibility. A nearby cemetery overlooking the valley feels thick with solitude—its simple white headstones marking the lives of nineteenth-century sisters who died in their twenties and twentieth-century sisters who lasted deep into their nineties.

The longevity of the sisters, coupled with the current shortage of young women entering religious life, has forever changed the complexion of this community. Of the roughly 135 women in residence at the motherhouse, 78 live in the infirmary—it has become a de facto nursing home. Part of the facility was recently sectioned off with an alarm system and locks to accommodate the growing population of sisters with Alzheimer's disease. At the time of my visit, the youngest sister there was forty—a rare brunette in a sea of gray at meals and Mass. She is heavily relied upon by the increasingly needy older sisters, so much so that she has to wear a beeper.

I drop in on Sister Margaret, who looks aged and frail in her delicate eyeglasses and upswept silver hair. For all the dolls, music boxes, and stuffed animals that are placed about, her room is depressing; it is a hospital room, after all, where Sister Margaret will live out the rest of her days. She spends much of her time in a chair by the bed, studying for her correspondence course in theology. Her aluminum walker is always within reach. Fluorescent green tennis balls are affixed to the bottoms of its legs, allowing her to propel herself more easily and less noisily along the slick floors. Infirmity prevents her from making it to the chapel for Mass anymore; instead Sister Margaret dials up a closed-circuit shot of the altar on her television, so she can attend services without leaving her room.

I have an automatic reaction to all of this. I feel pity for Sister Margaret, as I do for anyone facing the end of her life—especially someone who has missed out on so much: marriage, sex, children. I find myself wondering if Sister Margaret gets scared and lonely from time to time and if, in this chilly twilight, she ever questions the routine of zealous self-sacrifice that she consigned herself to, all those years ago.

I begin to tell Sister Margaret about my project: a book on contemporary American sisters and nuns, told from the point of view of a total outsider. The daughter of a Jewish-born atheist father and a lapsed Lutheran mother who has since turned to Zen Buddhism, I never belonged to a church and have no religious training; as such, I am curious about faith and the challenges of religious life. Sister Margaret listens to me with a quizzical look that I can't quite figure out but am used to, having explained myself so many times to prospective interviewees. But by the end of my speech her head is tilting from the sheer weight of bemusement. She is stuck on something I said at the very beginning. "You were raised with no religion? You didn't go to church?" She sits back in her chair, moving her head slowly from side to side. "I just can't imagine that," she whispers.

And with that, through some sort of divine sleight of hand, I became the pitiable one—hitherto youthful, hopeful me. How, she wondered, did I comfort myself in hard times? What did I believe in? Where did I find the strength to get up in the morning without faith? And with no belief in the great beyond, how did I view my inevitable death? Suddenly I saw Sister Margaret as ineffably content, buoyed by her righteous faith in something larger than I could ever imagine, delighted by the prospect of a glorious eternity in heaven. Her life had been a long tribute to that vision; to pity her would be absurd. By contrast, I was the one facing an uncertain future, with far more questions than answers.

Outsiders are forever being whipsawed in this fashion. Many of us view faith as a sign of weakness, uncomfortable as we are with the vagaries of the preternatural. We prefer our realities cold and hard. On the other hand, if someone's got proof of something amazing at work in the universe, we want in. Afterlife, the path to a richer, more meaningful life—in the deep recesses of our skeptical souls, most of us nourish some small desire to believe.

That desire has only intensified in an era where spirituality is the last frontier, the one remaining area of human experience that hasn't quite yet been thoroughly digested and exploited. From the blithely pornographic fare on cable TV to the regular reports of shootings in schools and office buildings, sex and violence are so public and commonplace it is almost impossible to shock us anymore. We see life as it happens—the air strikes, the car chases, the moment-by-moment fluctuations of the Dow. We are all horribly in the know. As a result, only that which is unknowable can still amaze us—only something as unfilmable and unquantifiable as faith. It is an excessive, heedless time, in which people capable of faith and restraint are startlingly unusual.

The more I thought about the way we live now, the more intrigued I became with the quiet strength of women who seemed untouched by trends, who toiled in the unremunerative realm of the spirit. Immune to the widespread and doomed push to superwomanhood, nuns had long been imagining brave new ways of being female in the world. Believers and crusaders, capable of extreme commitment in the land of divorce, they lived by a plan so grand it justified their giving up everything else. Although I knew next to nothing about nuns, it seemed clear that they were the pioneers, on a soulful mission that held the promise of real fulfillment.

How strange, then, to discover that—in this country anyway—they might also be heading toward extinction.

The American nun population reached its peak of more than 181,000 in 1965. Ten years later their numbers had dropped to 135,000. Today there are roughly 84,000, with a median age nearing seventy. Hospitals and schools founded by nuns are being sold, waning communities are folding, while convents that manage to hold on are buckling under the burden of caring for their elderly. Indeed, the greatest challenge facing most communities today is how to cope with their overwhelmingly geriatric populations and how to attract new blood to an institution seen as moribund.

What happened to deplete the nuns' ranks so drastically? Despite its vast achievements, the revolutionary Second Vatican Council of the early sixties was certainly a factor, as was the feminist movement—the gains from which undermined the notion that religious life was a realm of singular opportunity. For any number of reasons, in a very short period of time, American nuns began to question a way of life and a legacy that was nearly two thousand years old.

Today most nuns don't even wear habits. Many live in houses and apartments just like the rest of us. Without unique customs and a strictly circumscribed sphere of influence, why be a nun at all, especially now, with the institution unraveling? I wanted to discover who still chooses this life, what is essential in their experience, and what would be lost if their kind disappeared. My suspicion was that we were better off with nuns than without. In fact, maybe we needed them now more than ever.

When I was young, schoolmates often asked each other, "What are you?" Meaning, "What is your ethnic makeup, and in what religion were you raised?" My standard answer was "I'm nothing." It wasn't meant to be self-pitying, but rather a passable description of my patchwork ethnicity. It was also an easy way of avoiding the Jewish stuff, fearful as I always was of awakening anti-Semitic proclivities in the people of the quaint and deeply gentile Connecticut town where I grew up. New York, where I would ultimately move, is the ideal place for people who are "nothing." I have felt very at home here.

But my early brushes with Catholicism left their mark. As a child I attended my friends' first Holy Communions and listened to their weekly tales of Sunday school, presided over by kooky Mother So-and-So and Sister That-One. If I'd had a Saturday-night sleep-over at the home of a churchgoing friend, I often attended Mass with the family the following morning. On such occasions I suppose you could say I had my nose pressed up against the stained glass as I marveled at the rules and rituals that ordered the Catholic's life, rooting it in such a rich and fabled tradition. I envied what looked like a blasé belief in the unbelievable that was anathema in such a hyperrational family as mine (we simply had no experience with the drama implied by church names like Christ the King and Precious Blood—places Catholics went to as casually as to the grocery store). Powered by roiling emotions, tantalized by the prospect of a cushy forevermore in a place called heaven, Catholics had no room in their lives, it seemed to me, for boredom and doubt. Best of all, they belonged. That is what I envied the most.

As an outsider writing about nuns, I would have the chance to explore the inner workings of this fascinating club with none of the rueful ambivalence that seems to shadow so many Catholics their entire lives. But my journey would have its own challenges. The lives of nuns have never been an open book; traditionally, they have not been as visible as priests, those loquacious athletic coaches, civic leaders, and Sunday sermonizers who dropped in on parishioners for dinner. Given colorful renderings from Bing Crosby's breezy Father O'Malley in *Going My Way* to Karl Malden's scrappy peacekeeper in *On the Waterfront*, even non-Catholics have a sense of priests as disseminators of tough love, who are available and personable, up to a point. Nuns, meanwhile, seemed to be an ethereal cabal, bonded by secret customs and rites. Our knowledge of them began and ended with their mystique. They were elusive and private, despite their utterly conspicuous manner of dress—the veils, the flowing robes, clicking rosaries, and clanking crosses.

The full-regalia nuns have always been the most mystifying, like the one I'd been seeing for years in a train station on my commute. Ancient and stooped, shrouded in black serge, expressionless and motionless as a dashboard Virgin Mary, she proffered a begging bowl as the commuters rushed past. Occasionally a businessman would shoot a coin in her direction as if she were a toll taker on the thruway.

Nuns like this—how they lived, what they ate, where they slept—were such an enigma. The idea of asking this stern, otherworldly figure for a chat seemed unthinkable. Then one day as I was making my way swiftly through the terminal, I gathered my courage and slipped from the commuter stream. I approached the nun, whose face was obscured by thick, watery eyeglass lenses, and introduced myself. She smiled and the mystique vanished. In her thick accent the sister told me about growing up one of ten children in Italy and coming to the United States in 1938. She had been soliciting for the needy in the train station for two decades now, where even the occasional homeless person somehow manages to put a penny in her bowl. Not long ago she broke her wrist when a harried commuter accidentally knocked her to the ground. The nun was extraordinary in her ordinariness, kind of a nice old lady—albeit one who cleaved to an unspeakably harsh code, who lived every day swathed in the garb of a nineteenth-century widow. Why? What sustained her? What were the rewards in being a nun? But I would have to go elsewhere for my answers. The nun declined to sit for formal questioning, explaining that she was here to work. In her grim sphere, there is so much work to be done.

As I looked for women to talk to and write about, I aimed for a variety of experiences and backgrounds. I also sought out the grassroots laborers as opposed to media stars like the outspoken conservative Mother Angelica, whose fame has put her in a class by herself. My methodology was unscientific, to say the least. I called the aunts, sisters, and friends of friends who happened to be nuns; I cold-called schools and nun-run shelters, where most of the sisters were surprisingly welcoming, despite my embarrassing ignorance. To give you an idea of just how much an outsider I was when I began, I used the word "sequestered" when what I meant was "cloistered"—visions of robed women on jury duty leap to mind. The tolerant sister I was talking to at the time very gently set me straight. (Since then I have learned my terms: For instance, "nun" technically refers to a woman who has taken solemn vows, lives in the cloister, and devotes her life to prayer, while "sister" denotes a woman who takes simple vows in an active order focused on health care, the needs of the poor, and so on. But in this book I follow the common custom of using the terms interchangeably, in addition to the blanket term "woman religious." In the few cases where a degree of anonymity was requested, I use pseudonyms or omit surnames and other identifying details.)

As I spent time with nuns, my assumptions fell away, in moments and exchanges I never anticipated. At one point during my research I found out I was pregnant. With real—and in retrospect, idiotic—trepidation, I would go to interview nuns wearing baggy sweaters that obscured my belly for fear that they would disapprove of the sexuality that got me into this position (never mind that I am married). I imagined their discomfort with my being an older first-time mom, implying, as it might, a heavy reliance on church-banned birth control over the years. What I did not expect were all the pairs of nuns' hands that reached spontaneously for my stomach and all the conversations I would have about tilted uteruses and dilated cervixes with nuns who also happened to be nurses. I learned that nuns can be downright earthy, especially in the presence of babies. Loretto sisters swarmed my daughter, then ten months, when I visited their motherhouse. Once I was kissing her and bouncing her on my knee in the refectory as an older nun beamed at us from a few inches away. "You love her so much," she said with an approving smile. I had to agree. Then she added, "Just think how much Jesus loves her." My knee went still. It hadn't occurred to me; on the basis of what, exactly, would we even think so? But okay. That is what I was here to learn about, after all.

The occasional presence of my small daughter on these trips brought out in nuns a motherliness that I could relate to. In fact, upon reading yet another article about a priest who had sexually abused the children in his parish, I started picturing the nun as a savvy, protective mother figure who understands the problems and secrets of her brood, in contrast to a father who is out of touch at best and exploitative at worst. Indeed, the crisis in the priesthood— regular charges of molestation combined with steadily declining numbers—has encouraged many nuns to rethink their own roles and behave less like helpers than leaders.

Still, they are saddled with a strange and dated reputation, and some of them are getting tired of it. Upon meeting people for the first time, one former nun strenuously hides the fact that she was in religious life for almost twenty years, so weary is she of the preconceptions, questions, and judgments. Ironically, it is the preconceptions of respectful, well-meaning people that burden her the most. They seem to assume that because she is a nun, she is somehow better and purer than they are. Some religious are weary of the projected holiness and the automatic awe.

I wanted to put a human face to the institution; I wanted to paint a caricature-free picture of their lot. In recent years I have met scholars, farmers, activists, New Age enthusiasts, radicals, dancers, businesswomen, and adoptive mothers who all called themselves women religious. To discover who they are and what they all share beyond a few superficial common traits (like the love of a well-told joke and a virtual inability to leave food on their plates that would otherwise be shoveled into the trash), I had to look deeper. For their essential nature is something profoundly interior, and pondering that has been a new challenge.

As a magazine writer I have interviewed a number of actors—movie stars with glowing exteriors whose validation comes from someplace outside themselves. But the very richness of the image they are able to project for the camera is often matched by their ordinariness off-screen. Some are like Japanese lanterns: pretty, paper-thin, and empty inside. At a certain point I realized that the nuns I was meeting were exactly the opposite. Usually their exteriors are quite unremarkable, given their lack of vanity. Their complexities, their strength and inspiration all come from within, which I think is what makes a lot of nuns look as if there is something burning brightly inside them.

But that shine in the eyes isn't all devotion and tranquillity. I have seen nuns radiate real anger during conversations about the institutional church. I have grown accustomed to their hissing references to "Rome": absurd directives of one sort or another coming down from Rome; Rome dispatching cardinals to reprimand nuns; how out of touch Rome is with the issues faced by women religious. In such contexts "Rome" is a kind of ominous shorthand for the pope and the Vatican, that dark and faraway mission control. Some nuns are ferocious on the subject of the church's male hierarchy and its outdated refusal to let nuns grow and change with the times. Still others have spoken with bitterness and remorse about their own sisters and the role they think they have played in depleting the institution—compromising the essence of religious life in the rush to modernize. In a very real sense the battle is on for the soul of this institution.

Who is fighting this fight, and what, exactly, is at stake? To find out, I began by exploring the impact of the Second Vatican Council, also known as Vatican II. Then I took a close look at several aspects of the nun's life, beginning with the exterior business of appearances and moving inward to that mystical sense of being "called." I focus exclusively on Catholic nuns in the United States, and of those nuns, only a small sample. (It should be noted that American nuns' issues are unique. In much of Latin America, for instance, religious life is a growth industry, at least partly because women there still face a serious dearth of opportunities.) My aim is not to provide an authoritative and detailed account of women religious in the modern Catholic era. I leave that to the scholars and historians. My hope is to serve up the kind of fresh truth that comes with the outsider's capacity to be surprised.

I also wanted to find where nuns' lives intersect with ours, which was not hard. Like many laywomen, a lot of nuns have been motivated by a desire to do something important with their lives in a world that is skewed in men's favor. Although some would balk at the characterization, being a nun seems inherently feminist: This rigorous and communal life fosters a self-reliance and interdependence among women in spite of the patriarchy that oversees it. Even though I was becoming a wife and a mother as I began work on this book, I was sympathetic to anyone who didn't feel called to those roles and could brave the intense cultural pressure to fall in line.

On some level, then, For the Love of God is less a tale of the exotic than the familiar story of women emerging from the shadows, redrawing the roles that had been assigned to them, and then dealing with the consequences. Like the rest of us, nuns have been looking for the answers, the light, in a frequently dark and difficult life.

That said, theirs is a journey more ardent and fraught than

anything we could possibly imagine, especially for those who entered before Vatican II. Surviving the transition from medievalism to modernism was nothing short of heroic. Now, with that generation on its last legs, I wanted to capture the spirit of their struggle, before it is too late.

INTO THE WOODS

Vatican II

*I*N THE SPRING OF 1998, MARIE, A former nun, invited me to join her on a trip back to the Trappistine monastery where she lived for eleven years, some thirty years ago. The occasion was an open house—an opportunity for the sisters to show friends and family their newly renovated chapel, as well as a convalescent facility they recently had built. For me this was a unique chance to glimpse the inner workings of a monastery that is usually off-limits to outsiders and to converse with sisters who almost never issue invitations. But for Marie it was a bittersweet return to a time and place of incomparable intensity.

The Trappistines, otherwise known as the Order of Cistercians of the Strict Observance, were founded by a disparate group of religious women seeking refuge in Switzerland during the French Revolution with some Trappist monks who had recently fled France. Dating back to the twelfth century, the Cistercian way of life is a seamless cleaving to the Rule of Benedict—an incantatory prescription of seclusion, work, and prayer as envisioned by the sixth-century hermit for whom the Benedictine order is named. St. Benedict's aim was for an exquisite balance of work and prayer, along with an asceticism so total it would free the soul for an unobstructed communion with God. Today there are five communities of Cistercian nuns of the Strict Observance in the United States, whose considerable mystique derives from their dogged adherence to traditions that are fifteen centuries old.

The day sparkled as we drove up the turnpike through New England, to the expansive, tranquil farmland that surrounds the monastery. At many monasteries the chief activity after prayer has been farming, as it was in the days of their forebears. Of course, a well-run farm has enormous practical value, helping to keep the sisters solvent and self-sufficient (this monastery has sustained itself for decades with dairy cows and calves raised for veal). Working together also strengthens the bonds of the community, and community provides the essential structure of the life. For many monastics the grinding manual labor also enhances the ethereal business of contemplation and prayer, mitigating the psychological strain of living such an interior existence. The repetitive, often solitary nature of the work lends itself to reflection, and there is no such thing as a trivial chore. Whether pulling weeds or nailing boards, nuns and monks strive to bring a humble and openhearted perseverance to the work that mirrors their devotion to God. It hardly need be said that very few people are suited to such a regimen. As the eloquent Trappist monk Thomas Merton wrote in his book *The Silent Life*, "No one with weak nerves or neurotic tendencies should be encouraged to enter a Trappist monastery." The caveat clearly applies to the Trappists' female counterparts, the Trappistines, as well.

When we arrive, we go directly to the chapel, where a number of family members and friends have gathered to watch the sisters chant the office of none, one of seven daily interludes when prayer takes the form of voices lifted in song (together they are called the Divine Office). Amid the nuns' grueling daily routine, chanting the Divine Office is an experience of such uncommon exhilaration it is no wonder that some women are initially drawn to the life by the music. The nuns' voices, aided by the excellent acoustics of vaulted ceilings, strike a sound of inhuman purity and simplicity—fluttering like doves into the upper reaches of the building, surging and receding, trailing off in delicate unison, then gently disengaging for a celestial call and response. At various times during the Office the nuns stand in their choir stalls. On the underside of each seat is a small ledge, called a "misericord," on which they can prop their backsides when the seat is up and rest their muscles for a few moments. However fleeting, this is blessed relief, given the amount of time the nuns spend on their knees with their upper bodies extended extravagantly in prayer.

When the Office is over, everyone in the chapel bursts into warm salutations and smiles, making that strange, instantaneous leap between ritual and the real world that one experiences at weddings and funerals. People drift into the new medical facility, where cookies, cakes, and punch have been set up on tables. Such lighthearted fare for such a serious place—fully equipped hospital rooms anchored by a new nurses' station. I tell Marie I hadn't realized that the Trappistines also do some nursing. They don't, she explains. These facilities are for the sisters, most of whom are well into their seventies and eighties. Rather grandly for such a no-frills community, they are feathering their own deathbeds.

Overly animated nuns in white robes, black scapulars (the apronlike tunic that is layered over the robe), black veils, wide leather belts, and sandals are awkwardly herding guests to the snack table and giving brief tours, having found themselves in the unfamiliar position of playing hostess. Marie approaches a sister she used to know, looks deep into her eyes, and smiles. The sister is confused—Marie, after all, is dressed as they have never seen her, in khaki pants and a plaid shirt, her hair neatly done in a modern cut (this is the first time any of them have even seen her hair). The sister stares, then brightens and whispers Marie's convent name, still wondering if it is really she. They embrace one another somewhat formally; this is the traditional Cistercian greeting known as the "Pax"—a sign of peace and unity. "Where are you?" "New York." "New York? Everything's okay?" "Fine, fine, everything's fine." There isn't much more to say than this. Words have never been the stuff of their bond.

We go outside, where people are milling about, taking care to stay on the sidewalk. At monasteries there are invisible boundaries everywhere marking off areas that are considered the "enclosure"—the private domain of the sisters. Even though

Marie traveled the area around the barn hundreds of times with shovel and wheelbarrow, to traipse up there now would be grossly disrespectful, for she is not one of them anymore.

She smiles warmly when she sees two sisters from the old days coming down from the barn to say hello. One is wearing a denim work habit and smells strongly of manure. She and Marie shared a cell subdivided by a metal partition (each nun had her own sink). Customarily, one would rap on the partition to wake the other for early chores in the barn—early often meaning before 3:00 A.M. The other sister who comes down to greet us is a tiny Southerner wearing ski boots with her habit. She is a nun of special talents. Myth has it that she can actually hypnotize chickens—holding them by the scruffs of their necks and staring into their eyes, then laying them down on their backs.

I shake both sisters' hands. They are thick and strong and dry as husks. These nuns are the hard laborers who, along with Marie, entered the community as lay sisters—not to be confused with the choir sisters who sing the Office (and thus know more Latin than most lay sisters). At one time choir sisters also tended to come from families that could afford the thousand-dollar dowry required of them by the order. In an organization where mutual dependence and the spirit of community are all, many sisters chafed at this blatant classism.

The women embrace one another; much staring and smiling, even some giggling. The sisters remark on how good Marie looks, and it is true. Most of the sisters seem awfully gray and small, even bent by their ceaseless labors. Meanwhile, Marie, who by New York City standards maintains an exceedingly unflashy appearance, suddenly seems worldly and sleek to me, compared to these aging workhorses.

The women joke about the early days of getting used to the endless hours of making hay and milking cows. Sometimes it got so cold the holy water would freeze right in its cup, which was attached to a wall of the barn. It was the sisters' custom to dip in their fingers and make the sign of the cross upon entering, except on those mornings when their fingers hit solid ice. On such days, while milking, they would first tuck their hands in between the cows' udders and thighs to warm them up. It was inevitable that the sisters would develop a close relationship with the cows, leaning their veiled heads against the Holsteins' big, soft stomachs while they worked. In addition to milking them, the sisters midwifed their births. More than once when a calf was being born, it would take two sisters plus one of the Trappist brothers who lived nearby to pull it out by its forelegs and head.

The women laugh; they compare biceps—some of the sisters' arms might be thin, but they're like iron rails. Weaklings would never cut it as lay sisters. The relationships are still so fierce, all these years later—like those of men who fought in the same out-fit in World War II. No one else could ever really know what they have been through.

By late afternoon we decide it is time to go. Although I am a newcomer, saying good-bye feels a little strange, like tiptoeing across a plank connecting their world to ours, then knocking the plank into a ravine far below. It is unimaginable that the sisters, at this point in their lives, could ever cross the unfathomable chasm that separates us.

We get into our rental car. I say to Marie how nice it must have been to have a chance to chat with her former sisters, just like in the old days.

"That's the first time I've ever had a conversation with either of them," she says.

Although the rules at many monasteries like this one have been relaxed somewhat since Vatican II, silence remains fundamental to the Trappistine ethic. If the nuns need to relay information, they do so through Cistercian sign language. Catching me nonplussed at her response, Marie is quick to say that an absence of talk in no way keeps the sisters from communicating, nor does it necessarily hamper their sense of humor. Once, when the cardinal came to visit the sisters, as a special treat he granted them temporary permission to talk. At which point one nun turned to another and said, "As I was saying . . ."

According to the monastics, working side by side, day after day, year after year without the distracting clatter of small talk allows for a more profound kind of communication, with one another, as well as with God. Marie says it is what she misses most about monastic life—the silence.

For secular chatterboxes a community like this is a vivid reminder of just how wide of the mainstream some religious women fall and just how deep their traditions run. It also underscores what a loaded concept "change" can be. Not surprisingly, when the call for change rang out at Vatican II—an abbreviation redolent of smartness and speed, like the nicknames of race cars and rockets—a number of nuns were overcome with confusion. Their lives, after all, had been shaped by entrenched customs and seemingly unshakable beliefs. Women drawn to the convent were taking on a role burnished by history, shimmering with an inviolable sense of rightness.

Those old enough to have been buffeted by the changes of Vatican II entered religious life during a time when young girls didn't pass the hours calculating their futures and weighing their options. For Catholic girls taught by nuns in the twenties, thirties, and forties, going to convent school and then entering the novitiate as a teenager was a plan as reasonable and almost as common as a young woman's pursuit of a business degree is today. Virginal, naïve perhaps, and unconflicted, many women simply sailed into the life as their sisters and aunts had so assuredly done before them. For some it was almost like going into the family business. At the time the decision to become a nun was wholly apolitical and largely uncontroversial.

This was hardly the case in the eighteenth and nineteenth centuries, when European nuns started coming to America in real numbers to minister to the exploding immigrant populations. Given their foreignness and their strange, medieval customs, they braved considerable anti-Catholic prejudice. Often they were looked upon as something akin to witches; convents were burned and fancifully lurid tales of the life inside were circulated and read like pornography. In time, however, nuns' good works in schools and hospitals, and especially their courageous care of soldiers and orphans during the Civil War, went a long way toward quelling the prejudice.

The early memories of today's elderly sisters tend to brim with an unquestioning innocence. The hardest part, always, was leaving the family. Many parents were loath to give up their daughters—usually teenagers when they left home—to a life that consumed them whole, hiding them away for years at a time. In those days the decision to enter religious life had some of the dark valor and finality of joining the French Foreign Legion.

These were lifelong commitments that effectively severed a girl's ties to her past: Once in the convent, she jettisoned her family name in favor of a new, sometimes gender-obliterating one (often that of a male saint who, it was hoped, would watch over her and even intercede, occasionally, on her behalf). She would also don new garb, leaving the clothes of her former life hanging in a closet at home to be dealt with by her family, as if she had died. Even if a relative fell ill or an emergency arose at home, she was generally expected to remain with her new family, her sisters—a living witness to Christ's words: "Whoever loves father or mother more than me is not worthy of me; and whoever loves son or daughter more than me is not worthy of me; and whoever does not take the cross and follow me is not worthy of me" (Matthew 10:37–38).

Becoming a nun also kept a young woman from what used to be considered her primary duty, bearing children, and many parents had difficulty accepting that as well. A few nuns can recall the "Where did we go wrong?" lament. "I remember my father just looking at me with tears in his eyes and saying, 'What could we have done to make you want to stay?' " one sister recalls. The answer, of course, was absolutely nothing. She simply felt compelled by something even stronger than the love of her family. Difficult as that was, most Catholic immigrant families ultimately took pride in having reared a servant of the church; often, those with a brood would dutifully offer up one or two. Some felt it gave them a kind of "in," even though having a nun in the family conferred none of the prestige of having raised a priest.

Older nuns have vivid recollections of the sisters who impressed them as children; it was often a stern but loving teacher or parish sister who served as an attractive model of religious life worth emulating. Such women were at once fearsome and alluring to little Catholic girls—girls like five-year-old Joan McVeigh. Now in her sixties, an assistant professor of English at a community college in Chicago, McVeigh still remembers the first nun she ever spoke to, with the sunny recall typical of Catholic women of her generation. It was during the Depression in a town called Spalding, a small Irish Catholic settlement in the sandhills of Nebraska.

"My family ran a little dairy, and we delivered milk and cream and butter to the sisters," says McVeigh, whose Irish face has broad, strong planes and eyes that literally twinkle and disappear when she smiles. "Now, ordinarily I was not allowed to be anywhere near the buggy that we used, but somebody must have been sick, and so my brother took me to town with him to do some of the running. He gave me the milk and cream to drop by the convent. He said, 'Just put your finger on that button.'" In other words, don't lean on the doorbell, don't wait for the door to open, and for goodness' sake, don't linger or speak if someone comes. "I'd never seen a doorbell before," McVeigh says. "So I put my finger on the button and didn't take it off. He never said to take it off! So it kept ringing and ringing and ringing. And my brother yelled to me, 'Now you're gonna get it!'

"I'd seen the sisters at church," she says. "They were these wonderful women, these mystical creatures, with the black veil and white habit and the rosary that hung almost down to the floor. But I'd never spoken to one before. So I stood there, absolutely petrified. I knew my life was over. And then the door opened. This woman appeared—she almost filled the entire doorway. She came down, knelt, and said, 'What is your name? How old are you?' Then she took the milk and cream and said, 'It was very nice to have you come to our house' or something like that. Then she disappeared. I turned around and looked at my brother. I knew better than to sass him, but that was the first time I realized that big people didn't always know everything. From that time on I always really loved the sisters." Fourteen years later she became a sister herself.

To have a call was seen as something magical and nonnegotiable. Nuns lived in secrecy, separated from the real world by an awe-inspiring otherness. Many small-town Catholic girls who were drawn to the life at a young age never looked back once they had made their commitment, as ambivalence was routinely suppressed. Their constancy is astonishing, considering how overstimulated and distracted girls are today by all manner of media and mall.

It is hard to imagine the current climate producing someone like Sister Alban. She has been a Sister of Loretto for seventy-five of her ninety years. Living in the infirmary, when I visit her she is wearing a pink bed jacket and working on a quilt, each panel of which she has stitched with an Irish design (a leprechaun, a harp, an Irish flag, a map of Ireland). Manipulating the unwieldy yards of cloth can be difficult for a woman of her age, "like wrestling with a young colt," Sister Alban says with a hint of a twang. Not long ago the staff managed to wedge a quilting frame into her room, which has helped a great deal. Before, after an hour or two of sewing, "I'd be sweating like I'd just plowed the fields," she says.

Like most girls in her day, Sister Alban didn't torture herself assessing the pros and cons of becoming a nun. She grew up in

Kentucky one of eleven children, six of whom died young. Born Elizabeth House, Sister Alban was schooled by Loretto sisters and decided early on that she wanted to become one herself. "People always ask me, 'How did you know what religious life was? How did you know anything about it?' And I say, 'Well, I really *didn't* know anything.' The only thing I knew about religious life was that it was a way to give yourself to God, and that's what I wanted to do, regardless of what that meant." So on June 7, 1923, Sister Alban traveled by horse and buggy to the Loretto motherhouse, the same place she'd be living seventy-five years later.

For decades the life was uncommonly strict—Sister Alban says there was more silence in the Loretto community at the time than even among the intensely austere Carmelites. But the severity of the life never bothered her. "I don't regret any of that," she says. "It never seemed that hard to me, because that's what I was coming for."

What did prove difficult was having to hold jobs for which she had virtually no training. Just a few weeks after becoming a professed sister, Sister Alban found herself teaching school. At the time such unpreparedness was the norm. Sisters' schedules were so busy and regimented, it could easily take a couple of decades to complete an academic degree. Not until the Sister Formation Movement of the 1950s, which aimed at securing stronger education and preparation for sisters within a reasonable number of years, were they assured adequate training for their jobs (before this, nuns weren't even allowed to study theology; nor were they supposed to read the Bible on their own).

In Sister Alban's day, nuns simply marshaled their instincts and did the best they could with what they had (second nature for the pioneering Loretto sisters, who hold the distinction of being the first American Catholic women's order founded without a European affiliation). They also leaned heavily on God. "I thought, 'I have no business being in this classroom,'" Sister Alban remembers. "But that's what they told me to do"—meaning, that was the directive that came down from her superiors: to teach this grade at this school at this particular time. "I was a firm believer that obedience was the direct will of God—if you obeyed, He would help you out. And I thought, 'Well, God, this is Your job, not mine.'"

There is something unimaginably luxurious about the life Sister Alban describes. Who doesn't dream of shedding all anxieties and insecurities and completely trusting that somewhere, someone has a plan for you? How freeing it must be to place your worries in someone else's hands—hands as capable, presumably, as God's. Yet this system of belief seems incongruous with the enterprising spirit that religious life requires of nuns. To be so bold as to forgo the comforts of family life in favor of a strict religious community that would dispatch you to classrooms and hospitals with little warning and no preparation—by necessity, nuns of that time were fearless innovators. Yet those same women were so meek before God, so happily and instantly reduced to humble servants by what they believed to be God's will. Childlike, almost, in their desire to please Him. This duality is played out again and again in the lives of many sisters—women who created school curricula and founded hospitals, who also had to ask permission to stay up an hour past the convent's bedtime. "They made babies of us," as one former nun describes it. "The day I got my habit, my mother came to visit. I called her 'Mama.'

And Reverend Mother said, 'That's not your mama; *I'm* your mama now.' "

In Sister Alban's life that paradox was a leitmotif. Eventually she turned from teaching to nursing—a job for which she was equally ill prepared. "The first time a cancer patient was sent out here, I met the doctor out in the hall and said, 'Doctor, I want to tell you I don't know anything about medications,' " she remembers. " 'So you have to talk to me in plain English. I don't understand medical terms.' And he was wonderful to me. He taught me how to take temperatures and blood pressure and what to give. He taught me everything I knew. In this order I taught and I nursed, and I had no training for either one. But the Lord always took care of me." To hear her describe it, Sister Alban spent her days curled up in the palm of God's hand.

I ask her if in all of her seventy-five years in religious life she ever questioned her decision to become a nun. Did she ever, even for a second, think about leaving?

The blankness of Sister Alban's expression suggests that she is hearing the question for the first time.

"Never," she says. "When I came, I wanted to give my life to God, and I want to do it till I die."

To some, such an existence looks like a long exercise in blissful ignorance. Indeed, blind faith is anathema to the contemporary striver who is plotting his future and watching his back at once. But there is an enviable abandon in Sister Alban's total readiness to believe. A corrosive capacity for doubt isn't in her makeup; sisters like her are quietly bewildered only by the shortage of women willing to live such a graced and glorious life. And in that they are relics from another time entirely.

But that was the nature of it, before Vatican II. Nuns from that era often describe malt-shop crushes and the cute boys they'd left behind, recalling their youthful dalliances in such a lighthearted, sentimental manner; rarely do they betray anything even approaching regret. Such women simply surrendered themselves to a call that, at the time, felt inexorable. Either that or they just couldn't see themselves doing anything else.

"When I entered, there weren't too many choices," says Sister Donna Quinn, a Sinsinawa Dominican from an Irish Catholic Chicago family who took her final vows in 1960. "You could be married with children, you could be a nurse, or you could be a secretary. I wanted to be a nun. A nun and a teacher. I didn't want to be a teacher without being a nun. Somehow they were tied together for me." Probably because her own teachers had always been nuns.

Sister Donna says she knew she wanted to be a nun since she was five—"since I was able to think," she jokes, her Midwestern vowels stretched flat as she speaks, her deceptively impish face framed by loose, graying curls. As if following a winsome, fifties-era Hollywood script, she admits that young love briefly threatened her resolve. "I met this fellow before I entered and fell madly in love with him. And I thought, 'Oh, well, I'll go and then after about a month I'll leave. I'll just take the train home.' So I entered in September, and by October I was brainwashed!" She laughs.

Almost immediately Sister Donna was granted a reprieve: The superior of the community she was entering died the week before she and her class were expected. Since so many people would be attending the funeral, there would be no room for the new postulants. The girls got to spend an extra week at home. "So I ran home and called the fellow I was going with, and we went out dancing," Sister Donna says. But when she finally went to the convent, she stayed. She chuckles and beams at the memory, with no visible hint of wondering what she might have missed. As for the guy, he wound up marrying one of Sister Donna's best friends.

It is hard to reconcile such an innocent beginning in religious life with Sister Donna's post–Vatican II radicalism. As it turns out, she is among the most vocal of feminist nuns, whose confrontational approach has incited legendary fury among cardinals and bishops. In this she is like her good friend and comrade, fellow Chicagoan Sister Margaret Traxler, the daughter of a country doctor who became a School Sister of Notre Dame upon her graduation from high school in 1941. The decision to do so was pure and simple: There were scant alternatives for girls at the time, and Margaret admired the School Sisters who were her teachers. But religious life was anything but pure and simple. Sister Margaret became one of the harshest critics of the institutional church in or outside of religious life.

"Nuns are the victims of a patriarchal church," she says in a voice that is thick, soft, and low; when she's talking about the male clergy, Sister Margaret's whispery voice is tinged, like Clint Eastwood's, with barely contained hostility. "It's subtle, but it's bludgeoning. They're destroying the nuns. What young woman with a sense of social justice would put herself in a situation where a priest or a bishop could make her feel like a kept woman?" On the subject of the late Cardinal John O'Connor's opposition to gays marching in the New York City St. Patrick's

Day parade, she hisses, "Leave them alone! It was just his way of diverting attention from all the sexual abuse in the clergy." Having protested, marched, and cofounded the fiercely outspoken National Coalition of American Nuns, Sister Margaret is regarded by progressive sisters as a hero—even a legend, according to one. Told as much, she harrumphs and says, "Oh, honey, I'm just an old potato."

Surely Sister Margaret didn't set out to become a legend. But then, no one could have predicted the impact that Vatican II would have on the nuns.

Soon after Cardinal Angelo Roncalli became Pope John XXIII in 1958, he defied his putative role as short-term minder of the status quo when he announced his plan for an ecumenical council, the first since 1869. While the nineteenth-century council was notable for its unilateral assertion of papal infallibility, the aims of Vatican II, by contrast, bordered on the democratic. With unprecedented attention to the disposition of the laity, the council set out to examine the role of the Catholic Church in modern society and map out its direction for the future. The feeling was that at the rate society was moving, if the church didn't modernize and meet the needs of contemporary parishioners, it was doomed to irrelevance. At bottom, religious vows, missions, and commitments needed to be updated and renewed. The catchphrase of the council was "religious renewal."

Vatican II was comprised of four sessions held between 1962 and 1965. Catholic bishops from around the world were invited; more than twenty-six hundred attended. And for the first time in the history of church business, the faithful didn't have to imagine what was going on behind the Vatican's ornate walls. Television cameras recorded the proceedings, while astonishing images were beamed via satellite across the globe—images of bishops from a broad racial spectrum streaming into St. Peter's Square for that historic first session, their tall white miters bobbing like boats on a crowded river. Another first at Vatican II was the inclusion of women: Exactly twenty-three were invited to be auditors, only one of whom was an American nun—Loretto sister Mary Luke Tobin, who had recently been elected president of the Conference of Major Religious Superiors of Women in the United States. Assuming that neither she nor any nun would be invited, Sister Mary Luke had taken it upon herself to go to Rome and see for herself what was going on at the council. While in the middle of the Atlantic aboard a boat bound for Italy, she received phone calls from reporters seeking comment on her having been invited to Vatican II. Only then did she realize that she had been.

While the meetings produced a wealth of material—sixteen detailed documents in all—the boldest stroke of the council, with the most concrete ramifications for the ordinary churchgoer, was the repeated encouragement to cast off hoary, outmoded customs and make church rituals accessible to contemporary worshippers. Based on the recommendations of various Vatican II committees, some edicts were spelled out, while other proposals of a more general nature led to experimentation and interpretation in parishes around the world.

Probably the most dramatic step was the translation of the Mass from the traditional and largely inscrutable Latin into the vernacular of the realm. Now not only could all parishioners finally understand what was being said, they were given responses in their own language to exchange with the priest, along with new choreography of a sort, which invited a literal reaching out from one parishioner to another at a particular point during Mass. In addition, the altar was turned around to face the people. No longer did the congregation stare at the priest's back during Mass and passively observe his intercession on their behalf. Eventually, magisterial icons were crowded out by homemade murals and banners, while sermons became increasingly timely and political. The notion of what constituted church music also was expanded to include folk songs played on guitars and tambourines. And the laity's role in church services increased, to the extent that they assisted in the distribution of consecrated wine and wafers during Communion. The fourth wall in this holiest of theaters was disintegrating. The overall effect was one of startling demystification.

Many sisters, meanwhile, were receiving their paperback copies of the Vatican II documents and poring over them. Most community superiors were also minding the directive to lead their women in conversations about the documents, although some seemed to hope that by ignoring Vatican II, it would go away. In the book *Ex-Nuns* one sister writes of her community's efforts to keep the younger nuns in the dark: "They didn't want us contaminated by radical ideas. We used to steal position papers from the retired sisters' bulletin board in order to find out what was going on in the community. The habit was the hot issue."

Other hot issues were contained in the document called *Perfectae Caritatis*, the "Decree on the Appropriate Renewal of Religious Life." The challenge being put to women religious to reinterpret their customs in a more contemporary light was unmistakable in certain passages:

> The manner of living, praying, and working should be suitably adapted everywhere, but especially in mission territories, to the modern physical and psychological circumstances of the members and also, as required by the nature of each institute, to the necessities of the apostolate, the demands of the culture, and social and economic circumstances. Therefore let constitutions, directories, custom books, books of prayer and ceremonies and such like be suitably re-edited and, obsolete laws being suppressed, be adapted to the decrees of this sacred synod.

The implications were revolutionary. The church, which had long been thought of as eternal and fixed, impervious to the currents of history, was suddenly being characterized by the pope himself as an organic entity that should evolve with the times. Meanwhile, nuns, long resigned to the most arcane rules and regulations, were now expected to speak out, have opinions, and question their way of life. Even though the call to change seemed most applicable to women in active orders whose effectiveness in the field would surely be enhanced by an awareness of how people live now, contemplative orders were in no way exempt.

In some communities the mandate came as an unimaginable boon. "It was a fresh wind," says Sister Margaret Traxler, echoing Pope John XXIII's express desire that the council would function like the opening of a window, letting fresh air in. "It was like a spring day. There was a little chill, but you could smell the woods."

Indeed, many musty traditions needed to be aired out and ultimately discarded. Sisters had long been treated as mute handmaidens whose duties included keeping the priests comfortable and well fed. Never were they consulted on ecclesiastical matters of any import; nor did they have a say in the rules that shaped their own lives. So having to wear a heavy wool habit in hundred-degree weather went unquestioned in some orders, where sisters who had come from damp places like Ireland reported miserable, recurrent bouts with prickly heat. In some communities sisters weren't allowed to bathe more than once a week, in the interest of cutting down on nakedness and water bills; nor could they leave the convent to visit a gravely ill parent or write or receive letters without the mother superior's censoring them first. Busy teaching sisters were expected to adhere to unreasonably early curfews, originally mandated in the days before electricity, when moving about in the dark was just plain unsafe. Such rules were wisely reconsidered, as was the notion of extreme cloistering. In Julia Lieblich's book *Sisters* a nun remembers seeing a woman fall and hurt herself outside the cloister, but the rules against leaving the enclosure were so strict that none of the nuns would go and help her. "We were so scrupulous, we would not cross the threshold. Fortunately, a doctor came by to visit the chapel and found her."

Inside, postulants (first-year candidates) weren't allowed to talk to novices (fiercely tested, often segregated soul-searchers who have pledged first vows), and novices weren't allowed to talk to professed sisters (full-fledged nuns who have pledged final vows). "It was so weird," says one former nun. "You had to walk with your eyes down and your hands in your sleeves. And if you were a postulant and a professed sister was coming down the hall in the opposite direction, you had to stop and stand by the wall until she passed. You didn't say 'Hello.' We had a greeting—'*Laudetur Jesus Christus*'—Praised be Jesus Christ. You never said 'Hi.' " The emphasis on self-abnegation in some places went so far as to forbid the use of the word "my," implying, as it does, ownership and possessions. "So," says one unsentimental former nun, "we had to say things like 'Mother, our robe is frayed.' What's next? 'Our Kotex needs changing'?"

Public humiliation was a widely used technique before Vatican II. During the weekly ritual called the Chapter of Faults, sisters had to confess their infractions against the Rule of the order in front of all their sisters, at which point the superior would mete out some sort of punishment. For instance, for failing to complete a chore a sister might be made to lie on the floor in the chapel or the refectory where the nuns took meals, thus forcing the other sisters to step over her—a pointed illustration of how the failings of one can inconvenience the group. Perhaps the punishments were administered with the best of intentions, and maybe the rules were even fortifying on occasion. Still, it is no wonder that some of the young women reared in these traditions went on to punish schoolchildren arbitrarily and sadistically. Without question, abuse, including the self-inflicted kind, can occur in organizations where suffering is highly valued.

The notion that a nun had to be hollowed out—her spirit broken and her sense of self demolished—before she could be filled up with Christ was an early casualty of Vatican II. For the first time in their consecrated lives, sisters were being encouraged to share their opinions and feelings with their community. For many it was a terrifying proposition. It simply ran counter to the tradition in which they had been trained—a tradition of obedience, stoicism, and, in many cases, silence. Some found themselves attempting to wrap their minds and mouths around concepts theretofore banned from their psyches.

The ability to adapt was required on every level, and especially on the profound level of what it meant to be a sister. For centuries the feeling prevailed in monasteries and convents that there was something sullied and secondary about secular life, that the vowed life was truly a superior existence. In his 1954 encyclical *Sacra Virginitas* ("On Consecrated Virginity"), which underscores the importance of remaining virginal for God, Pope Pius XII said, "[whoever] argues that it is preferable to live in matrimony than to consecrate oneself completely to God, without doubt perverts the right order." Similarly, it was felt that the nun's time on earth was negligible in every sense, compared to what awaits her in heaven—which explains onetime macabre practices like covering nuns with a funeral pall on the occasion of their solemn vows, or the Loretto tradition of maintaining an open grave at the entrance to their chapel as a reminder of the rich reward that awaits after death. But with Vatican II came the bold notion that all are called, albeit to different things, and that a secular call is nothing to apologize for. While such an idea greatly validated lay labors, there were nuns who felt that it devalued the mission for which they had given up everything.

Still, many communities found themselves swept up in the spirit of change. It was hard to resist, as the impulse to question and rethink established patterns had gripped the country. Just outside the convent walls the din was rising from the women's movement and the civil-rights activists, while anti–Vietnam War demonstrations voiced the sort of outrage that most sisters found difficult to ignore. One former nun who was attending Catholic University in Washington, D.C., at the time says she could barely get to class without stumbling on an antiwar protest pleading a message of peace to which she was inherently sympathetic. Eventually she and several other sisters in her community felt it their duty to join in. And in 1965, when police on horseback clubbed civil-rights marchers in Selma, Alabama, the word went out among women religious that something had to be done. So nuns from communities all over the country boarded planes and flew into the fray, standing arm in arm with black protesters and facing down state troopers. Of course, some communities refused to allow any of their sisters to go, uncomfortable as they were with the volatile and worldly realm of politics. In a sense Selma foreshadowed the incipient splintering of women religious along political and ideological lines.

To take such public stands was largely unprecedented for American nuns. But never before had they felt so justified. In the first place, the ethos of Vatican II gave credence to the notion that nuns actually held worthwhile opinions. In addition, nuns in the sixties were better educated than at any other time in their history, thanks to the strides made by the Sister Formation Movement. Now, in college and graduate school, they were being exposed for the first time to catalytic theological concepts, like those in the works of the thirteenth-century philosopher and theologian St. Thomas Aquinas. Few notions in all of theology would have a greater impact on the life of the modern nun than that expressed in St. Thomas's *Summa Theologica*, which essentially said that the ultimate authority in moral issues is one's own conscience.

For progressive, freethinking nuns, that belief, coupled with the spirit of individualism that suddenly coursed through the nation, gave them license to disagree with the Vatican on a host of issues, from birth control and abortion to the ordination of women. Belief in the primacy of personal conscience cleared the way for the kind of heated and highly politicized dissension that no living nun had ever before witnessed. Furthermore, as individuality is essentially at odds with the aims of community, a cornerstone of religious life was coming loose.

For some nuns this was a disastrous turn of events. Those who were drawn to religious life for the security, the predictability, and the inviolable system of belief it seemed to promise did not want to hear that the rules and answers were not, in fact, fixed. Still other nuns rejoiced at what they took to be a humane and long-overdue acknowledgment of their ability to decide things for themselves. For these nuns the world events tempting them to activism coincided nicely with the churchwide mandate to rethink archaic customs. Suddenly rules like the ban on newspapers, magazines, and unsanctioned books, which ostensibly aimed at keeping sisters' minds clear for contemplation and prayer, bordered on the ridiculous; in some communities such customs were quickly terminated. As the thinking now went, in order to exercise personal conscience intelligently, sisters had to know what was going on in the world.

But sisters who felt a jubilant sense of promise in the wake of Vatican II were not unaware of the storm clouds gathering. In the first place, the exodus was hard to miss. Whether emboldened or embittered by the changes, nuns in great numbers began leaving their communities. In cloistered orders the epidemic of vanishing sisters was not a topic for discussion. But it was obvious in the refectory. A missing sister's plate and utensils would remain in place for a while, "then even those would disappear," as one former sister remembers. In some active communities it was actually announced over dinner that a particular sister would not be returning. "It got to the point where I had a pit in my stomach waiting for the next announcement," says a Daughter of Charity whose continuation in religious life required a serious period of grieving for those who had left. It was as if they had died, when in truth it was religious life as the nuns knew it that was passing. "Our whole community just kind of thundered apart," according to one Franciscan sister. "We disbanded the novitiate. We kind of told people, 'Just go home. We don't know who we are. And if we don't know who we are, how can you join us?' "

"They left big holes in our hearts," Sister Joan McVeigh says of all the women who had abruptly opted out. "And it seemed that the women leaving were the liberals, the leaders, the creative ones, making us wonder if we were the dumb-dumb sisters staying behind." But some of the creative ones stayed as well, eager to refashion religious life from top to bottom. Operating on a loose and very American interpretation of "renewal," their enterprising plans didn't sit well with the Vatican. In certain communities experimentation drew the sort of angry rebuke from church elders that belied the openhearted spirit of Vatican II. No one felt it more fiercely than the Immaculate Heart of Mary sisters in Los Angeles, whose extensive experimentation with their rules and customs included the early abandonment of the habit and traditional forms of communal prayer. The archbishop of Los Angeles at the time, Cardinal James Francis McIntyre, became so enraged by the sisters' actions that he encouraged a Vatican investigation of their community. Ultimately the sisters were ordered to stop their bold improvisations. And when the community's request for an appeal went unanswered by the Vatican, more than three hundred of their four hundred sisters left religious life altogether to form their own secular community.

It was a watershed moment. To this day, the Immaculate Heart of Mary sisters are invoked as martyrs by progressive sisters. But the strangest part of that story was the archbishop's apparent belief that the command to cease and desist would somehow pull the sisters back in line. As everyone involved would soon see, there was no turning back from Vatican II.

CLOTHE MY SOUL, O LORD

The Habit

The religious habit, an outward mark of consecration to God, should be simple and modest, poor and at the same time becoming. In addition it must meet the requirements of health and be suited to the circumstances of time and place and to the needs of the ministry involved. The habits of both men and women religious which do not conform to these norms must be changed.

From *Perfectae Caritatas*

NO ONE INVOLVED IN THE DRAFTing of that statement could have imagined the agonizing controversy it would unleash. For embedded in such seemingly simple ideas was a vast amount of room for interpretation—especially in the loaded notion that habits should be adapted to the needs of various ministries. Although habits are becoming increasingly scarce, they remain the most vivid symbol of Vatican II upheaval.

The issue of the habit is unique in its visibility. While the typical parishioner isn't likely to know or care if a particular community has decided to allow a little small talk during meals in the refectory, many lay Catholics were watching the changes in religious dress as carefully as was any nun. A Texan in her forties recalls how upset her mother was by the disintegration of the habit, as she felt almost like an accessory to the crime: She did seamstress work for the local parish. And when the time came to hem the robes to the knee and the veils to the shoulder, she felt as though they were literally hacking away at who the nuns were and what they stood for. An Irish Catholic in his fifties well remembers the sound his parochial-school teachers made as they moved through the halls. Despite his being an exceedingly lapsed Catholic today, he wistfully says, "I miss the swishing and the clacking." With its belled sleeves that hid pitch pipes, rulers, clickers, tissues, arms, and who knew what else, the habit embodied some of the dark mystery of faith itself. It is intensely evocative; it was and remains a strong statement. Even non-Catholics have gut reactions to serge-draped sisters out in the world, as well as to women in street clothes who turn out to be nuns.

Our Lady of the Rock Benedictine Priory is located on Shaw Island off the coast of Washington State. Traveling there from the East Coast is a punishing journey, involving an eight-hour plane ride from New York followed by three hours on a van to the town of Anacortes on the forested coast of Washington. There you pick up the San Juan ferry and sail for another hour into North Puget Sound before finally reaching tiny Shaw Island, population 160. But in the end it seems appropriate that the trip be so long and hard. The Benedictines inhabit another century, after all, and the voyage puts significant physical and psychological distance between them and modern civilization.

The lowing of a foghorn and waves stroking the dock echo in

the night as the ferry pulls in, easing its way between enormous timber pilings as the mechanical dock slowly drops like a jaw. Some laywomen are there to transport me to the monastery, as the nuns' rigorous regimen prevents them from coming out at this hour. Swerving to avoid tree branches that had been scattered across the road by a violent wind, we drive to Our Lady of the Rock.

The next morning the back door of the guesthouse swings open, and a robed figure fills the frame. It is Mother Hildegard George, swathed in a tunic and scapular involving several yards of a drapey black cotton blend. Her round, wind-chapped face is cinched by a white wimple and topped by a long black veil. The wimple is a severe, unforgiving apparatus, blocking out the hair as it does, putting the wearer's face in a perpetual state of peekaboo. But its whiteness also shows off Mother Hildegard's periwinkle eyes. The robes drape softly over what looks like a strong, rounded physique underneath.

Mother Hildegard throws wide her robed arms, fabric cascading, reeling me in for a hug, even though we have never met. As it happens, hospitality is a cornerstone of Benedictine spirituality. "All guests who present themselves are to be welcomed as Christ," Benedict advised back in the sixth century. He also encouraged that "the abbot or prioress shall pour water on the hands of the guest, and the abbot or prioress with the entire community shall wash their feet," although the Rule of Benedict isn't always taken literally, most guests are relieved to learn.

The daughter of a prosperous California architect and a onetime professional opera singer, Mother Hildegard entered the Benedictine community in 1969. What followed were ten unmerciful years of formation at the Benedictine abbey Regina Laudis, located in Bethlehem, Connecticut. The abbey was founded by Reverend Mother Benedict Duss, an American who was educated in France and received a medical degree from the Sorbonne. After becoming a surgeon, she entered a Benedictine monastery in France that was occupied by the Nazis during World War II. When General Patton's troops came to liberate the region, Mother Benedict—sequestered in the belltower—was overcome by the sight of the courageous soldiers. And when she saw the Stars and Stripes that adorned their military trucks, she took it as a call from God that she should return their gift by establishing a contemplative community back in America. In 1946, she and another nun traveled to Bethlehem to begin that long process. Over thirty years later a laywoman visited the monastery and felt a powerful pull to the place. She converted to Catholicism and entered the community, of which she is still a member today. The woman is General Patton's granddaughter.

It seems there is something strong in the water at Regina Laudis, and Mother Hildegard is further proof. She is what you might call a pistol. "I'm a hooker," she once told me with a wink, referring to her skill in hooking pillows and rugs. Awfully talkative for a contemplative nun, fiercely opinionated, funny, and smart, she waves off politically correct notions like so many gnats. One day as she was strolling along the beach, she couldn't help but grunt as she peered up at an eagle circling overhead. "You'd think the Dalai Lama lived up there, the way you can't get near them or make any noise," she said. Over the years the eagles have swooped down and stolen some lambs from the nuns' flock, which might account for Mother Hildegard's disdain. "And of course you can't kill them," she said. "I said to Mother Prioress, 'I'll shoot 'em now and ask questions later!' "

She holds a doctorate in child and adolescent psychology. At one time Mother Hildegard considered becoming a child psychologist, until she realized she could help only a handful of children that way. By contrast, the number of lives she could touch through prayer is potentially limitless. It is but one of many mildly shocking notions Mother Hildegard puts forth so casually—shocking to the outsider in their sheer implausibility. One pictures her prayer being transmitted to God like a signal to a satellite, where it disperses into infinite wavelengths of grace that are then beamed into the homes of troubled children all over the globe.

But even the nonbeliever can be inspired by her unapologetic faith in the essential rightness of the old ways, which found people cowering before God. Never would they dream of doing anything as disrespectful as, say, wearing shorts to church. "We relaxed so much after Vatican II," Mother Hildegard says. "So it kind of became 'Christ is our brother and we are all one.' Well, I'm sorry, folks, He's also the savior. Do you realize what you're doing when you go to Mass in shorts? And people don't. They fulfill an obligation, and then they're on to the next thing. I'm so sick of everything being watered down. I'm getting to the point where I think only prayer can save us." Her staunchness is invigorating, as is her loyalty to a life that finds her knee-deep in manure when she is not actually down on her two bum knees, beseeching the Lord, enclosed in a community with seven other nuns and a priest who lives in a trailer nearby.

Mother Hildegard, who is in her fifties, has a feisty edge of necessity. To stay a course like this in the post–Vatican II era is a struggle, particularly in garb that stamps her a reactionary—garb as conspicuous as a sandwich board and almost as uncomfort-

able. "Coming from Southern California, you never wore anything on your head," Mother Hildegard says. "Even in the days
when you had to wear a hat to church, I always wore a mantilla.
So for me, being wrapped up all the time is more confining than
I'd like." The garb can also be cumbersome. "My first Easter here,
one of the lambs got caught in the fence, and when I went to pull
his head out, the wind caught my veil and tore a rent about that
long. Well, thank God I didn't have my consecration veil on. But
there isn't anything I can't do in the habit: I've horseback-ridden,
and I used to ski every day. And when you stop and think of the
pioneer women, they did more than we've ever done." In a society where technology is utterly geared toward lessening waiting
time and reducing manual labor—where no one with options
accepts inconvenience without a fight—Mother Hildegard's
breezy truce with daily discomfort is bracingly old-school.

She accepts the discomfort because she sees a higher purpose
in her hard life, and especially in the wearing of a habit. This
afternoon she is sitting on the steps of the barn, a quarter mile or
so from the enclosure where she and the other nuns live. The
interior of the enclosure is strictly off-limits to laypeople, unless
the nuns need help hoisting something large or changing a lightbulb that is out of reach. As she talks, a cagey llama named
Bravo, with whom Mother Hildegard seems to have a love/hate
relationship, coquettishly circles her, checking her out under
extravagant lashes, his velvety lips quivering toward some
foliage. Plaintive mooing drifts up from a lower meadow, home
to a few rare Scottish Highland cattle with long, wavy pelts, han-
dlebar horns, and eyes the size of boiled eggs set in leathery sock-
ets. "I can tell you, especially when I go to conferences, I
sometimes go to bed exhausted because so many people have

come up to me. I mean, you run into kooks once in a while," Mother Hildegard says. "But basically it's good people who are hungry for information or prayers. And if you don't have a habit on, how do people know who you are?"

Her argument sounds reasonable, but from Mother Hildegard it is an odd rhetorical tack. Her vocation is hardly what one would call apostolic; for the most part she is not in the soup kitchens or the hospitals or the inner city, serving as a visible symbol of Christ. Although she does teach catechism and participate in workshops and conferences around the country, most of her days are spent in a private world with the same handful of people, all of whom are well aware of her vowed status. In such a context a habit seems as superfluous as an elaborate wedding dress for a bride who is eloping. But the issue of the habit isn't that simple, as I would come to learn.

Lucky for Mother Hildegard, there is no latent love of style or fashion to test her allegiance to the habit. "I have naturally curly hair, and it was the bane of my life," she says. "For about fifteen years I wore it in a ponytail. Then one day I couldn't stand it anymore, and I just chopped it off. I've had it short ever since. My mother and her sisters were fashion plates, and I don't know if I got too much too soon, but it never meant much to me. I was really the bane of my mother. She had one girl and it was me— everything she didn't want in a daughter." Mother Hildegard quickly amends that thought. "She certainly was a great mother, but . . . I just was never that close to her."

As Mother Hildegard talks, her wimple starts to gape—to the point where some flesh around her neck becomes visible. On someone so painstakingly swathed, even a little skin can be startling.

The next day Mother Hildegard hops in the community's four-wheel-drive Subaru holding a big go-cup of coffee. She pulls in her habit before yanking the door shut. With errands to do on the mainland, she heads off to the ferry, navigating the narrow roads "faster than any guardian angel can fly," as a local friend of hers worriedly puts it.

Out here in the world of perms and tight jeans, the habit suddenly seems so dramatic; this is where it tends to have the greatest impact. But sometimes it is not the desired impact. Mother Hildegard brings some skeins of wool spun by the nuns into a shop that will sell them for her. The proprietor cocks her head toward a racy red Firebird in the parking lot and says conspiratorially to an unamused Mother Hildegard, "That yours? Ya trading up?" In a health-food store Mother Hildegard asks the woman behind the counter for help. "You want to confess something to me?" the clerk says with a grin. Both women, while friendly, seem a little patronizing—to them a nun in a habit is a vehicle to a punch line.

In the hardware store Mother Hildegard hopes to find feed bowls for the dogs and a soft duster on a long stick for their elegant new chapel—a pristine sanctuary made of sixteen kinds of wood including walnut, oak, western maple, and cedar, trimmed with a smooth, tan wood called madrona. A bamboo grille separates the pews from the choir stalls and the altar. (For years the women prayed in a damp and drafty grotto located beneath the monastery, reminiscent of the cave in which St. Benedict laid his spiritual groundwork.) As Mother Hildegard approaches, a teenage girl minding the register looks at her warily, her eyes traveling up and down the robes. Rather than ask if she can be of assistance, the girl appears rudely dumbstruck. Given Mother Hildegard's abundance of intelligence and savvy—both of which would have served her handsomely in the secular world, had she chosen to live there—it is strange to see her cast in the role of the suspect oddball. In this last case anyway, the habit proves far more repellent than magnetic.

In theory the habit is a reasonable convention. For women with more important things on their minds, the habit obviates time in clothing stores and in front of mirrors. Being relieved of the cost of a wardrobe also supports the vow of poverty, while the figure-obscuring, body-insulating fabric might, in some small way, enable the vow of chastity. Out in the world, the habit can also transmit a spiritual message quickly and efficiently. Even though Sister Margaret Traxler enthusiastically shed the robes the minute her community allowed it, she has firsthand experience with the power of the habit. On that frigid day in March of 1965 when she flew to Montgomery and then drove another sixty miles to Selma, she was led to the pulpit of a Baptist church and asked to speak about why she had come. Earlier she and several other habit-wearing nuns had formed a line of resistance in front of the billy-club-toting state troopers. Other activists fell in behind them and began singing protest songs. In its sheer symbolic weight, the face-to-face confrontation between placid, righteous nuns and dumbfounded troopers anticipated that indelible scene from the march on the Pentagon a few years later, when an antiwar protester slipped a flower into the barrel of a National Guardsman's rifle.

Along with sending a message, a prescribed code of dress can also foster the spirit of community that is elemental in religious orders. Save for the distinction between choir sisters and lay sisters, as well as among postulants, novices, and fully professed nuns, habits have the leveling effect of any uniform. Generally speaking, no one is elevated or cast out on the basis of her background and social status—biographical tidbits that are usually telegraphed in the lay world through the quality of one's clothes. When everyone in the community is wrestling with the same complicated outfit, the opportunities for empathy are limitless.

Yet even a decade before the start of Vatican II, during the papacy of Pius XII, the subject of religious dress was under scrutiny. For the issue of the habit turns on a fundamental irony. In the earliest days women religious in some orders wore long, dark robes in solidarity with the poor. The nuns' clothes approximated the colorless, unfitted, undecorated garb of the peasants. Yet as clothing styles changed, nuns, in allegiance to their foundresses, did not. For centuries they continued to use expensive, hard-to-find buttons and closures and dangerous steel pins, as the foundress had stipulated. So what had once been considered common, humble attire eventually was seen as exotic plumage, aggrandizing and glorifying its wearer, separating her from regular folk.

In her book *The Cloister Walk*, Kathleen Norris quotes the sixteenth-century Carmelite mystic Teresa of Ávila as saying, "Thank God for the things that I do not own." That wonderfully droll sentiment prompts Norris to write, "I could suddenly grasp that not ever having to think about what to wear was freedom, that a drastic stripping down to essentials in one's dress might also be a drastic enrichment of one's ability to focus on more important things." The problem is that the habit, as designed and worn in many orders (excluding the Benedictines that Norris knows and chronicles so richly), was anything but stripped down. The habits of some orders required such excessive swathing and capacious draping that the sisters looked less like spiritual servants than beekeepers or plutonium handlers. The

Religious of the Sacred Heart wore a bonnet with fluting of Eliz-
abethan proportions around the edges that framed their faces
like paper wrappers holding petits fours.

Even comparatively modest habits could be an ordeal. Consider the uniform of one Dominican community in the fifties: a
T-shirt, underskirt, a deep-pleated dress with wide sleeves,
undersleeves that prevented glimpses of arm flesh, a scapular, a
bandeau (the hair-hiding piece fitted to the forehead), a cowl,
and a veil. Not only did such an outfit require complicated maintenance that diverted sisters from more spiritual endeavors, it
was also uncomfortable and sometimes unsafe. In the days long
before central heating, the thick yards of cloth had a purpose in
keeping nuns reasonably warm and dry in dank convents. But in
the modern era—and in balmy climates and active ministries
never imagined by the orders' European foundresses—the habit
left nuns hobbled and sweltering (in some communities the sisters put a layer of paper toweling beneath the upper part of their
habits, as constant laundering was neither viable nor allowed).
The floor-length robes collected dirt and dustballs, and the
starched, face-encasing serre-têtes worn in some orders were so
tight they created sores and abrasions under the chin. For nuns
whose work required them to operate machinery or spend a certain amount of time behind the wheel of a car, the billowing
sleeves and blinkering veils posed a serious safety hazard.

The psychological stress of achieving the look of a nun went
well beyond learning how to assemble the habit. In many orders
women parted with their tresses the day they received their new
garb. In others, the nuns were instructed a day or two later to
report to a designated cell somewhere in the novitiate where
haircuts were being given. As if having just left one's family forever were not hard enough, imagine seeing great hanks and curls

tumbling to the floor, and razors running up the back and sides of young women's heads. In her 1975 memoir, *The Courage to Choose*, Sister Mary Griffin offers a shocking glimpse:

> In the dim light of flickering vigil lamps at Our Lady's shrine, I could make out the gleam of scissors, the large willow baskets lined with sheeting, the bent heads of the postulants as they buried their faces in cupped hands. If your hair was long enough, it hung in two thick braids to make the cutting easier. If short, it was pursued in a series of artless forays that left the victim skinned and somehow shamed looking. After the first few cuttings, I couldn't watch any more. The sound of snipping shears, the strangled sobs of a few less Spartan postulants seemed to signal the end of youth and laughter, the end of beauty, the yawning of the dungeon. Thus did one separate oneself from the love of things seen and give oneself utterly to the love of things unseen. I fingered my own cropped head and felt that there should have been a death bell tolling.

Disturbing as the experience of being sheared could be, a cool dispassion for such frivolous things as coifs and a willingness to wear one's hair very short became signs of a woman's commitment to her new life. Only the ambivalent felt the need to steal glances of themselves in the covers of their tin sewing boxes or in the panes of glass in the chapel doors as they repeatedly wiped them clean.

Despite the habit's onerous dimension, the prospect of a style change troubled many sisters for whom the habit provided a link to a centuries-old tradition. It was more than mere fabric, after all, having been blessed by the bishop during the dressing ceremony. In some orders it was customary to kiss each piece of the habit before putting it on and saying a prayer: "Clothe my soul, O Lord, with the nuptial robe of charity that I may carry it pure and undefiled before thy judgment seat," said the sister of Mercy of the Union while pulling on her habit. Describing the curious dressing ritual in her memoir, *Nun,* Mary Gilligan Wong talks of "taking care never to let any part of the consecrated cloth touch the floor": to that end, a strip of black tape had been sewn along the bottom edge of the habit skirt, just in case. The habit was a visible testament to a nun's devotion to God. It was also a rich symbol of the order in many cases, the disappearance of which led to an identity crisis for some of the sisters.

No sisters boasted a more identifiable habit than the Daughters of Charity, a French community founded in 1633. Requiring five yards of fabric, it involved a skirt, a kind of wide-sleeved tunic, an apron, and a starched white collar, topped with a cornette: gravity-defying headgear that resolved itself in dramatic points that protruded nearly a foot or so from either side of the head, earning the sisters the nickname "God's geese." (A version was worn by the Flying Nun of the 1960s television series.) Achieving the effect was no small feat; the cornette was fashioned of a double piece of rectangular linen, which was starched and dried, very straight and smooth, on zinc plates. Then it was folded and manipulated and pinned, its shape facilitated by a caplike piece underneath.

When Vatican II arrived, one did not have to search hard for reasons to dispense with the cornette: Its maintenance and preparation were time-consuming, it obscured the sisters' vision, and its unwieldy width caused the sisters to bump into windows and doors. Furthermore, it was obsolete, having been designed as a sunbonnet for the French peasant women who were the original Daughters. Sunstroke is not much of an issue for the urban

Daughters in St. Louis or elsewhere. Still, the cornette was a cherished artifact—a symbol recognized throughout the world. For
many Daughters this old habit would die hard. One Daughter
had been so excited about the prospect of eventually wearing the
cornette that she pasted a picture of one onto her own graduation
photo, which she then displayed at her going-away-to-the-
convent party. "But," she said, "my great-aunt, who tends to be a
little superstitious, said, 'A bride should never picture herself in
her wedding dress before she gets married, or she'll never wear
one!' " Her great-aunt was right. The cornette was dispensed
with shortly thereafter.

It happened in 1964. All at once, on September 20, the forty-
five thousand Daughters of Charity around the world took off
their cornettes for good, replacing them with boxy, face-framing
headgear (which was later replaced by a simple coiffe, or veil).
Sister Germaine Price, the assistant to the provincial in St. Louis,
remembers that as a very dramatic time—photographers even
came to take before-and-after pictures (after, it looked as though
the entire order had been caught in a downpour). Sister Germaine was teaching then, and the reaction of the students was
memorable. "It was like they were sort of embarrassed to look at
us because it was so different," she says. "Because the cornette
had given us so much added height, one of the things that was
really remarkable to the students was how short we all looked.
So many said, 'Look at how little they are!' We all suddenly
became much smaller in their minds." Smaller not only in the
physical sense, perhaps. Once the mystery and drama of the cornette disappeared, the sisters themselves must have seemed
shockingly earthbound and all too human.

Even progressive sisters find it difficult to dismiss the genuine

thrill of having donned robes that rustled with history and mystery in equal measure. "The day that I got the habit, I was wearing a black skirt, a white blouse, and a black veil," Sister Joan
McVeigh remembers, of the solemn ceremony in which a novice
takes her first vows. That is, she comes a step closer to being a
full-fledged nun. "Then the skirt, blouse, and veil were removed
by someone who is your dresser"—a professed nun—"and the
habit is placed on you." Generally this happened out of sight,
after which the women made a dramatic return in their new
regalia, while awed friends and family watched from the pews.
Sister Joan mentions the scene from the 1965 movie *Cat Ballou* in
which the gunslinging Lee Marvin is ceremoniously outfitted for
battle. "And that's how it felt," she says. "Kind of a Don Quixote
thing. Awww, it was marvelous."

It wasn't uncommon for Catholic girls to fantasize about the
garb. While others played dress-up in their mothers' slips, one
young sister-to-be was "playing nun"—losing herself in the oil-
stained overcoat that her grandfather wore to his manufacturing
job and cinching it with a leather belt, wearing a sheet on her
head for a veil. After all, nuns were said to be "brides of Christ,"
and there was plenty of room for matrimonial fantasy in the
gownlike habit, replete with shy, virginal headgear. A child at the
time, ecclesiastically ignorant and spiritually naïve, the sister-to-
be nonetheless sensed the specialness of religious life through the
drama and pageantry at the heart of Catholic ritual.

For along with the crucifix, the tabernacle that houses the
"body of Christ," the ornate chalice that holds the consecrated
wine, the bishops' tall miters, the incense and the bells ("smells
and bells," as the ironic and lapsed would have it), habits have
contributed to the inherent theatricality that is such a large part

of the faith's appeal. One socially liberal Catholic who never attends church anymore still feels proprietary of the church of his youth—of the incomprehensible Latin Mass that drove him into a deep and searching silence, of the humbling sermons and the awe-inspiring rituals. By contrast, the post–Vatican II Mass has all the spiritual uplift "of a Democratic fund-raiser," as he likes to say. In the opinion of many parishioners, the shedding of the habit has had a similar effect on nuns, humanizing and democratizing in a way that diminishes them.

But the sisters who jettisoned the habit usually had good—even profound—reasons for doing so. Some had grown uncomfortable with the unearned sanctity the robes seemed to confer. Upon seeing a sister in a habit, some people behaved as if the Virgin Mary had just materialized before them. According to one very humble sister in her seventies, when she was living in El Paso, Texas, strangers on the street actually would pick up the hem of her habit and kiss it. "I'd think, 'Oh, these dear people, probably holier than I, and here they are crawling around on the floor,'" she says with a sad shake of the head. "I'd think, 'If you only knew whose habit you were kissing.'" Indeed, the nun beneath the habit was often consumed by its stultifying mystique.

Perhaps women could have managed the habit more easily if they were relieved of it occasionally. Priests, for instance, have long been allowed to disguise their clerical status by removing their collar or simply putting on a sweater for routine forays into the lay world. But nuns could never be anything but nuns, having to bear up at all times under the weight of the robes and everything they implied. An honor, perhaps—the noblest of burdens, but a burden nonetheless. Some felt that this unyielding emphasis on how they should look, as dictated by all-male church elders, was typically and inherently sexist.

At a certain point some nuns couldn't help asking themselves, "Am I what I wear?"—especially when they received preferential treatment from strangers in lines and restaurants. Such favoritism flew in the face of the humility and sacrifice that supposedly defined the nun's life. "It became a symbol of privilege, rather than what St. Dominic meant it to be," says Sister Joan McVeigh. She remembers a cashier in a busy grocery store inviting her to come to the front of the line. "I was embarrassed," Sister Joan says, "but I knew she would insist. Well, nothing was won for the kingdom that day, as I walked past about six people and paid for my milk."

But Sister Joan also remembers a time when the habit functioned as the perfect tool of her ministry. She was sitting on a bus when a soldier—a Marine—came and took the seat beside her. He asked if they could talk. "The usual parochial stuff was exchanged," Sister Joan says. "He had attended St. Something school and had been an altar boy. He confessed shyly, as is often the case, that he did not go to Mass much anymore, but he remembered Sister So-and-So and he got a great education. Finally he fell silent, then asked if he could ask me something. I imagined it would be whether he was going to hell for not going to church or for eating meat on Friday. Instead he asked me if he would go to hell for murder.

"He mentioned that he had killed civilians in the Vietnam War, in village searches when the civilians were not distinguishable from the enemy. While I was completely opposed to the war, I knew that he did what he had no choice in doing, insofar as he believed his government in much the same way he believed his parochial-school sisters who taught him to live decently. His sadness was so terrible, and I know that the time we spent together was not a cure. But I could see that he was relieved, if only temporarily. I hope I gave him some strength to live with the personal hell he brought home from that gloryless war."

If Sister Joan hadn't been wearing a habit that day, they never would have had the conversation.

The logistics of amending the habit in the aftermath of Vatican II were predictably complicated. Religious communities were expected to meet and discuss their attire—along with every other aspect of their religious life—then experiment, submit proposals for change to Rome, and wait for approval. Of course, Rome did not respond promptly to every bit of business put forth by every community. But for many sisters change could not wait. In no time veils started to shrink, robes metamorphosed into skirts and scapulars into jackets, while entire habits in other communities disappeared altogether, replaced by a pin or gold ring that signified one's commitment to God. While in the old days you could spot a sister at a hundred paces, now you would have to squint and search for some sort of sign. But the strangest part was the staggered pace at which various sisters within the same community would accede to the changes. Some clung to the habit as long as possible, while others were quick to cast off what they saw as the remnant of a less enlightened past. The result was a kind of patchy molting: Communities that once were bonded by uniformity now saw a ragtag assortment of styles on sisters whose affiliations and relationships to one another were no longer so apparent.

A fair number of sisters would just as soon have stayed in the habit. But as lay clothes infiltrated, they began to feel conspicuous and a little lonely. Some said they were pushed over the edge when they realized they were being treated differently than lay-attired sisters. Indeed, habits were suddenly seen as a tip-off to the sisters' political leanings, vis-à-vis the litany of divisive issues that arose during the post–Vatican II era. In a conservative gathering, lay-attired sisters were ignored, while in a progressive group of people, nuns in habits were looked upon as the enemy. One former Sister of St. Francis recalls the chilly scene in the refectory during meals: When a sister walked in, heads turned and glances cut toward her hemline—especially if it was a hemline on the rise. Everyone wanted to know how everyone else felt about the prospect of life-altering change that was in the air, and hemlines were seen as a fairly reliable indicator. "I remember very well the bitterness of some of the older women," she says.

For the nuns who took the leap into lay clothes, the disdain of conservative sisters wasn't the only problem. As most of them entered the convent before ever having a chance to live on their own, they were not practiced in dressing and grooming themselves. Mothers and sisters of the biological kind made and sent clothes and offered guidance, but much of it was lost on the nuns. "It was comical," says Sister Joan McVeigh, "because we didn't know anything about setting hair or anything like that. Some sisters would just take the rollers out and that's the way they'd leave—going around with these little soft rolls all over their heads. At least I had sense enough to comb them out!" Others were uncomfortable showing their legs; the feel of the breeze on shins and calves for the first time in decades was hard to get used to. Some nuns had permanent creases in their cheeks and foreheads from years of wearing stiff, tight caps and wimples. And no one knew what to wear. "I had no sense of style," Sister Joan remembers. "None of us did. And much of our clothes came from clothing drives: If it fit, you took it. So we might wear a plaid with a stripe with flowers. Gradually we figured it out. You'd think, 'What she's wearing looks nice' or 'Oh, I see— brown jacket, brown skirt' "—Sister Joan scrutinizes an imaginary woman standing before her. " 'Oh, I've got it! Brown shoes, too!' It was laughable, but we finally figured it out." And although most nuns didn't know what to wear, many knew what not to wear: anything black. After the habit, some had a visceral aversion to the hue.

A number of nuns had no patience for such trivia. One elderly Loretto sister remembers receiving advice from the people she worked with in a school in Illinois. "They said, 'If you're going to change, you have to wear makeup,' " she says. "So they got me some Cover Girl rouge. I did that for about a week, and then I thought, 'Oh, this is stupid.' My complexion isn't good, but that never bothered me. That's not why I came to religious life—for my complexion! So I ditched that and went about my work." In the end, no matter how hard nuns tried, they were hopelessly short on the time and money that vanity demands. Ironically, the disintegration of one uniform would give rise to another: Soon enough, the durable, inexpensive, and mystique-free polyester pantsuit became the unofficial garb of the post–Vatican II sister.

While a small fraction of the nation's nuns still wear the habit, the debate in some circles has in no way disappeared with the robes. To this day some nuns judge one another harshly on the basis of their choice of outfit. "Oftentimes you'll meet a religious out of the habit and she won't even approach you," Mother Hildegard says. "They just don't even want to talk to you if you're in a habit. That's kind of a common thing. Sometimes I think they feel guilty, or they just feel they don't want to get involved with someone they think doesn't understand what they're doing. I don't know where they're coming from. It's very uncomfortable sometimes." Even in circumstances where no hostility exists, the diverse and personal clothing choices of otherwise like-minded sisters raise questions. At the Catholic Center in New York City, I've had lunch a few times with two administrators there—one in a knee-length habit, the other in lay clothes. And while I have enormous respect for their right to make their own choices, it always strikes me as odd. I find myself itching to say, "Why can't you all get together on this?" But I stop myself. For I have witnessed enough mild resentment on the part of sisters confronted by unsolicited opinions about what they should wear—opinions held by people who have never experienced the habit, let alone religious life. What annoys some of them most is all this hand-wringing emphasis on what, for them, are superficialities.

For those who still wrestle with the issue of the habit, the central questions always are, What is its purpose and whom is it for? With cloistered and semicloistered women like Mother Hildegard, its primary purpose has little to do with laypeople. The Benedictine habit is utterly consistent with the simplicity and austerity of monasticism. The way it is cared for and worn also fits right in with the ritualistic warp and woof of this profoundly structured and communal way of life. Like any other task at a monastery, the painstaking putting on and taking off of the habit provides women with regular opportunities to reflect on the nature and purpose of their commitment. And when prayer and work await, there is no time for cocking a hip and staring dreamily into the closet, wondering what would go well with what. One day as Mother Hildegard walked the windy beach—her sleeves and veil flapping as she searched the sand for shells that might make nice gifts—her garb and how she wore it radiated a kind of defiant beauty.

Then there are the nuns who say the habit is not for them but for the laypeople—laypeople like Sister Joan McVeigh's Vietnam veteran, who saw comfort and possibly salvation in the robes. The Daughters of Charity who once sported the cornette eventually began wearing a modest veil and knee-length blue skirt that have all the mystery of a candy striper's pinafore. But in a way that suited their straightforward, grassroots vocation. Fanning out in impoverished areas as soldiers in God's army, bringing comfort and services to the sick and disenfranchised, they are recognized on the street as the embodiment of charity. Neither figureheads nor proselytizers, they represent help for people in trouble, like a red first-aid cross or an emergency phone. As one former Daughter of Charity puts it, when you are wearing the habit and a homeless person staggers toward you, crossing to the other side of the street is not an option. You must find a way to help. "The habit called me to be the best person I could be," she says.

Still other nuns have been equally motivated by the needs of the laity in their decision to shed the habit. The idea was to make themselves more accessible and to live in solidarity with the humble and the poor, just like the robed sisters of centuries ago. Perhaps more than anything, nuns who put the habit behind them were moved by a desire to join the world—to live no longer like curios inside a bell jar. And they were confident that joining the world wouldn't make them any less a nun. Such sisters say the loss of the habit refocused them on the less tangible, more essential elements of their vocation. Even without the tip-off of the habit, sometimes a nun is unmistakably a nun: something in the smile, in the discreet way the woman occupies space. Sister Joan McVeigh relishes those times when someone just comes up to her and says "Are you a nun?" " 'How'd you know?' I say. 'I don't know, there's just something about you!' Now, *that* is when you're a nun," she says, savoring the notion and smiling so wide her eyes disappear. "No habit. It's just who you are."

And yet concern persists in other quarters that one of the great draws of religious life is vanishing. Many sisters admit that it was the habit specifically that attracted them to religious life in the first place. Recalling the period when she was shopping around for an order, one semicloistered postulant says she wouldn't even consider those that have done away with the habit, so elemental is the garb to her interpretation of the life. Meanwhile, potential candidates are unlikely to have their interest piqued by the nun on the street, who in most cases is indistinguishable from laypeople. With their numbers dropping, and with most of the remaining members going around incognito, sisters are disappearing, both literally and figuratively.

So it goes, say some sisters. Recruitment isn't their job, and attracting new members is a silly justification for wearing or doing anything. Besides, if recruitment is really the problem, there are other ways. As one good-humored sister recently suggested, how about lapel pins that say ASK ME ABOUT BEING A NUN!

It is easy to be charmed by the romantic throwback garb of a Mother Hildegard. Still, for many, there is something suspect about uniforms, with their suggestion of a kind of zealous separatism and subversion of self to the ideals of an organization. Depending on the circumstances, that can be dangerous. Even in some of the best-intentioned organizations, conformity is usually a cornerstone, as rugged individualism threatens cohesiveness and consensus. Such conformity comes at a price. Consider the word widely used in religious orders to describe that period in which a postulant and then novice is tested and groomed for religious life: "formation." It implies that the woman is stamped and shaped, her quirky edges trimmed and discarded. Surely the habit is intended to accomplish much the same.

While the aim of Vatican II may not have been to turn nuns into rugged individualists, its rhetoric encouraged respect for the unique gifts and opinions of the individual. But how could that square with the template of obedience that is the nun's life? A life lived in service of the Catholic Church, no less, which will never be mistaken for a democratic institution. If nuns charted their own course and dressed and lived as they wished, what, if anything, would still make them nuns?

DOING SOMETHING BIG FOR GOD

Nuns' Work

*I*DLENESS IS THE ENEMY OF THE soul," St. Benedict wrote. It is a lesson most nuns take to heart, judging from their tireless capacity for work, which they view as a gift from God. But the notion of what is the most soulful and necessary kind of work varies widely from order to order and from nun to nun. For instance, some nuns teach. Some nuns raise cattle. And some nuns—a very few—actually work in the circus. In the United States today there are nuns who belong to an order called the Little Sisters of Jesus, who fulfill their vocation in the Carson & Barnes Circus.

Headquartered in Oklahoma, Carson & Barnes is what is called a mud show—a five-ring extravaganza that is assembled in a field and taken apart in the space of a day. The company arrives in a city at dawn, does a day of performances, then packs up everything—the sixty thousand-square-foot tent, the basketball-playing bears, clowns, aerialists, concession stands, reptiles (OVER 100 FEET OF SNAKES! OVER 1,000 LBS OF SNAKES!), elephants, llamas, lions, and tigers—and presses on to the next city for shows the following day. Less famous than the Big Apple Circus or Cirque du Soleil, Carson & Barnes is a businesslike operation where Latin American and Eastern European immigrants have found a place to ply their dangerous trade.

The smell of dung, cotton candy, and hay lies thick about the grounds surrounding the vast red-and-white-striped tent. Inside, Miss Maigo is on the cloud swing and the Mercedes sisters are on the so-called aerial perch—all in small, glittering costumes, smiling existentially as they kick their legs, flop backward, and twist their upside-down bodies high above the gasping crowd. Later on, dalmatians in frilly collars ride miniature ponies, while tigers perched on platforms are coaxed with a whip into a begging posture. The Flying Salazars and the Flying Cavallinis are warming up, along with a quartet of stoic young men who will be trying their luck on the "Death-Defying Double Wheels of Destiny." At one point during the show, elephants process around the perimeter of the tent, tail to trunk, in thundering silence.

It is hard to imagine where the nuns fit in. But they are here. Outside the tent, working the souvenir stand, is a woman conspicuous for her absence of any traces of showmanship. She is wearing jeans and a circus T-shirt, with graying braided hair pinned up in the back and what could only be called nuns' eyes: greenish brown in her case, welcoming and sympathetic, with fanning creases at the corners that are undisguised by makeup. More to the point, she is wearing a wooden cross with a tiny red heart at its center on a thin cord around her neck.

She is sitting behind the table on which she sells Carson & Barnes buttons, pennants, T-shirts, and hats, as well as "friendship rocks"—ordinary stones spray-painted gold (two for twenty-five cents). A sign explains: ONE TO BE TREASURED, ONE TO BE GIVEN AWAY, LIKE THE JOY AND WONDER YOU FOUND HERE TODAY. The stones represent an unlikely bit of enterprise on the part of the nun, who collects them herself on the circus's behalf, admitting with a weary smile that some visitors cry, "Rip-off!"

Her name is Jo Byrne. In the late seventies, at the request of the order, she and another Little Sister, Priscilla Buehlmann, set about trying to establish a prayerful presence in the circus, just as some European Little Sisters were already doing (Priscilla among them, until relocating here). After researching circuses, they set their sights on Circus Vargas, a California-based outfit that happened to be performing in Florida. To get there, they had found a vehicle through a drive-away program in Washington, D.C., where one drives a car to some destination that the owner can't or doesn't want to take it to himself, and gets a free trip in the process. The car they ended up with was a Mercedes—very fancy for nuns on a meager budget who were still wearing habits at the time (a denim dress, leather belt, and sandals). They heated whatever food they had on a Sterno stove they kept in the back of the car.

That was the easy part. When the sisters arrived in Florida, the circus had already gone to Galveston, Texas. So they set out on its trail in a borrowed car with bucket seats that were a nightmare to sleep in, and by the time they reached the circus, it was getting ready to go to Phoenix, Arizona. Told that even if they were allowed to join, there were no accommodations for women, the sisters remained undaunted. With money from the order, they bought a used van, while a friend of Sister Jo's mother gave them a trailer. When Sisters Jo and Priscilla arrived in Phoenix, they were finally put to work sewing costumes and repairing elephant blankets, as well as selling hot dogs, cotton candy, popcorn, and soda out of the Candy Wagon. They stayed for eight years. After several years with two other circuses, they joined Carson & Barnes.

The lengths the sisters went to in landing their jobs seem a bit outrageous—even for sisters, who are a generally tenacious breed. On the surface there certainly doesn't seem to be any especially religious dimension to circus life. Even if there were, Sisters Jo and Priscilla aren't performing any particularly religious functions here, aside from maintaining a chapel in their van. But if you have given yourself over to the Little Sisters of Jesus, a life in the circus makes perfect sense.

The order was founded by Magdeleine Hutin, a Frenchwoman with a wide, strong face and tunneling eyes who would come to be known as Little Sister Magdeleine of Jesus. Born in 1898 to a military doctor and his wife, one of six children, she had lost all of her siblings to either illness or the First World War by the time she was twenty. Magdeleine suffered her entire life with tubercular pleurisy, a disease so compromising it threatened to prevent her from living out her religious vocation. The feeling that she was destined for spiritual service intensified when she read a biography of the visionary French priest Charles de Foucauld. Espousing a life of devotion and contemplation amid the poor and abandoned, Foucauld fulfilled his own vocation while living with the Muslim nomads in the Sahara. Magdeleine couldn't imagine a more gratifying existence—her father had served with French troops in North Africa and developed an affection for the people there that may have rubbed off on his daughter. But her infirmity was so debilitating she was continually warned against traveling and taxing herself.

Ironically, it was Magdeleine's poor health that ultimately led her into the life she had dreamed about. While serving as head-mistress at a Catholic girls' boarding school in France, she was diagnosed with a crippling form of arthritis. Her doctor told her that the only hope she had of arresting the ravages of the disease was to live out her days in a place where it never rains. A place like the Sahara Desert, Magdeleine realized.

It was 1936. Almost immediately she boarded a ship to Algeria, where she would settle with the destitute, tent-dwelling desert nomads. With an eye to the practices of Charles de Foucauld, she was intent on sharing the hardship of the nomads' life by experi-encing it alongside them. Sister Magdeleine talked of being "the leaven in the dough"—of living as Jesus did, with and in total service to the poor—and the fact that the nomads were Muslims and she a Christian ultimately didn't matter. She wasn't inter-ested in converting people but rather in living as a contemplative out in the world: carrying on that intimate and constant dialogue with God amid harsh circumstances, bringing an empathy and a charity worthy of Jesus to the most forsaken people. People who are here one day and gone the next, people without a home. That simple prescription became the raison d'être of the Little Sisters of Jesus, the order she founded in 1939. True to the profound humility of the order, Little Sister Magdeleine described her wildly courageous spiritual journey like this: "God took me by the hand and I followed Him blindly."

Today there are Little Sisters of Jesus throughout the world. Some live a nomadic life while others have settled in permanent communities in strife-ridden neighborhoods. Although their global order numbers about thirteen hundred, there are only about twenty-five Little Sisters in the United States. A handful have been living in an impoverished pocket of Chicago's West Side since the late fifties. In 1969, during a confrontation between two gangs in a nearby alley, a stray bullet struck and killed one of the Little Sisters as she slept. The neighbors who had grown to love the nuns were heartbroken: Not only were they mourning the loss of Sister Dorothea, they assumed that the tragedy might scare away the remaining sisters. But while the sisters were deeply shaken by the incident, they recognized that this was what they'd signed up for. The idea was to be with the people and live their life—that is, suffer their pain and live as vulnerably as they do. If stray bullets were a part of life in that neighborhood, the Little Sisters accepted that. So they gave Sister Dorothea's habit to another nun roughly her size and carried on.

Elsewhere in the world, the Little Sisters' allegiance to nomadic people has drawn them to wandering populations such as Gypsies and, at one time, shepherds, while Sisters Jo and Priscilla make their spiritual home among those theatrical itinerants known as circus people. In the tradition of Little Sister Magdeleine, Sisters Jo and Priscilla are by no means the resident soul-savers at Carson & Barnes. They are prayerful workers who maintain a chapel primarily for their own use, although everyone is welcome. Once, when an elephant accidentally killed a clown who had come too close, the sisters were a welcome presence during the memorial on that full-moon night, as friends lit candles, left mementos, and shared stories at the site of the awful accident. The nuns also call upon their network of priest friends around the United States and schedule Masses, usually for special occasions like Easter, a baptism, or First Communion. "I really think they are a tender spot," as one of the Carson & Barnes clowns once put it. "They have a softening effect [on] a very hard-nosed, rough-and-tumble business."

Back at the circus, Sister Jo is joined by another nun, Sister Anne Beth Boucher. She is the "regional," whose job it is to check in with the Little Sisters in her area and provide whatever help and support they might need. Her long red hair is pulled back. She wears glasses, casual clothes, and a floppy hat with sunflowers on it. She is in her late thirties and could easily be taken for a local mother or girlfriend. But as she climbs up a small hillside not far from the big top and submits to some questions about her life, it becomes clear what a peculiar world she inhabits.

"We try to be closer to the people by living where they live and also by working at the same sorts of jobs they do," Little Sister Anne Beth says against the din of generators and squealing children roughhousing all around her. She has a gentle, intense, kind of rueful quality about her—a curious world-weariness for someone still so relatively young. Her sentences bubble up softly, in little surges, then recede. It's as if she is speaking in verse. "I worked for a year in a fast-food place—I've done that a couple of times. Burger King, McDonald's. I worked in a day-labor agency where they bus you to a factory. They have a certain number of full-time employees, and then they hire a certain number of temporary people every day. This was an Avon cosmetics factory. I lived in North Carolina for eight and a half years and I did factory sewing. I cleaned houses, worked in warehouses. Another sister cleaned rooms in motels and worked in a Wendy's. She also worked in a stereo-speaker factory."

It is difficult to understand what the purpose of the work was. Why flip hamburgers when you could be ministering to the sick or teaching or praying in a chapel? Where do those key elements of spirituality and service come in, and how does this idea of being contemplative out in the world really work? Sister Anne Beth tries to explain.

"Living a contemplative life means that you want to be that meeting place between God and people. So you spend time with God in order to bring Him to the people. And then you spend time with the people so that when you come to that place before God, you have them inhabiting you. You try to make that as concrete as you can: When you work with people, when you go to the Laundromat and meet them there, or on the buses or on the street corner waiting for the bus, or on the front steps in the evening when it's too hot to go inside—it's a way of concretely being one with the people."

Which isn't to say she is necessarily sitting around talking about God with her neighbors on buses and stoops, just as Little Sister Magdeleine didn't try to convert the Muslims. She is open. "But it is hard in the big city, in neighborhoods where people are afraid and look at you like you're crazy when you try to talk to them. It takes a long, long time—you have to look for every little opportunity. You stop and talk to people on the street; you try to go to the funerals when you know there's a funeral." To what end? To be there, to share their problems, to bear witness.

I ask Sister Anne Beth if it is ever difficult to blend the contemplative and the worldly lives. The latter certainly requires a measure of gregariousness, does it not? "Inwardness is an aspect even of gregariousness," Sister Anne Beth says, in her aphoristic way. "Being contemplative is listening and being aware in everything you do, including meeting people. A lot of Little Sisters find that aspect very difficult, and they really have to force themselves to go out" and interact with strangers. "Then there are some who are very outgoing who find it hard to find the discipline and the time to be silent. But you discover that both aspects need each other to be authentic. All human growth is a question of attaining balance. We all have natural tendencies in certain directions, and maturing means developing other tendencies so we have balance."

In her community in Baltimore, Sister Anne Beth and the sisters she lives with have organized prayer together, but their work schedule makes it hard. "Work is becoming more and more something people want you to do twenty-four hours a day, seven days a week, even Sundays," she says. "There are no nights anymore. It's a pagan society. So it becomes more and more difficult. Especially the jobs that are more menial—the work can often be after hours." They try to pray in the morning when everyone's fresher, or later at night, when the neighborhood is settling down and it's a little quieter.

To people who worry about the very real and practical problems facing the poor, the aims of the Little Sisters might seem absurdly low—Magdeleine saw the Little Sisters as being like bubbles let loose by Jesus, floating here and there, bringing some small joy. But there is a kind of poetic subtlety to their mission. Ambition doesn't even enter into it: Such a self-centered, performance-oriented impulse isn't likely ever to resonate with a Little Sister. And what they do isn't without its power. That simple but profound idea of bringing comfort to a person by immersing oneself in his or her circumstances—when you are in trouble, it is the difference between the person who heaps on the advice and the person who really empathizes. The former might yield more long-term benefits, but the latter is infinitely more satisfying to the soul.

I am reminded of a scene I witnessed at a nun-run homeless

shelter where I volunteered for several years. My job usually consisted of bringing full plates from the kitchen out to the homeless women—the ladies, as we always called them—in the dining room, then retreating to the kitchen door to stand and wait for more ladies to arrive. One loud and friendly volunteer had a wonderfully light, instinctive touch with the ladies. Unlike the rest of us, who might spoon some vegetables into a coffee cup at the end of our shifts and eat and small-talk with the sisters in the kitchen, this volunteer startled me one night by taking her dinner into the dining room. Wearing a big smile, she approached a table full of homeless women—women so relentlessly accustomed to being shunned—and asked if she could join them. They made space for her. Then the volunteer dug into her food and started chatting. No counseling, from the looks of it, no probing questions, just chitchat. One woman with a drug problem who regularly nodded off at meals kind of perked up. Soon the other women were listening, contributing. Laughing. I have no idea what they were talking about; I was watching from the kitchen door about twenty feet away. All I know is that the volunteer's natural, spontaneous decision to cross the threshold between us and them if only for the duration of a meal was one of the most graceful gestures I'd ever witnessed.

Similarly, the Little Sisters don't set lofty goals of the quantifiable sort; they are not social workers. Their purpose is rooted in the distinctly unsecular notion of just being, as openly and lovingly as possible.

While all sisters are expected to have a peaceful, private dimension, the Little Sisters are uncommon in their formal blending of contemplative and active approaches to religious life. Typically, sisters see themselves as one or the other, which, in turn, utterly determines the structure of their day and the nature of their work.

In 1633, Vincent de Paul and Louise de Marillac were ahead of their time in their founding of an apostolic community, the Daughters of Charity, which was the first successfully unenclosed community of religious women. De Paul, a French priest, founded relief organizations—or "charities," as they were known—intended to help the poor. In Paris the widowed de Marillac joined in his efforts by focusing on the urban poor with the help of humble, willing country girls. She brought them to live with her in the interest of mutual support. Eventually the idea came up of formalizing the arrangement by taking vows and making a permanent commitment to the cause, but de Paul had already seen similar efforts result in swift and punitive cloistering. So this time he found loopholes, instituting measures that distinguished the girls from traditional nuns, such as pledging private vows for a year at a time as opposed to the lifelong kind. So while today's Daughters are not considered to be nuns in the strict, canonical sense, their foremothers pioneered an archetypal form of consecrated life.

Along with helping the poor, nuns also found a ministry of almost limitless demands and scope in the realm of education. In the United States the legacy of the teaching sister dates back to their earliest days in this country, since the staffing of schools was one of the main reasons they came here. An adventurous spirit was every bit as important as the ability to teach, judging from the experience of the fabled Society of the Sacred Heart. In 1818 a handful of Sacred Heart nuns traveled from France to America with the intention of establishing the Society in the States. After a turbulent eleven-week voyage across the Atlantic on a ship called the *Rebecca*, they sailed into the Mississippi River

and anchored off New Orleans, where they were lowered in arm-
chairs into a dinghy and brought ashore. A few months later,
after traveling upriver, they established their first American convent and boarding school in St. Charles, Missouri. Out of such
rugged beginnings an elite tradition grew: Girls from the nation's
wealthiest and most prominent families would routinely be sent
to the precise, inscrutable Religious of the Sacred Heart at one of
their many palatial academies, for a regimen of refinement that
went well beyond academics. It was no ordinary time, as Mary
McCarthy made clear in *Memories of a Catholic Girlhood*:

> I looked upon my religion as a branch of civics and conformity,
> and the select Sacred Heart atmosphere took my breath away.
> The very austerities of our life had a mysterious aristocratic
> punctilio: the rule of silence so often clapped down on us at
> mealtimes, the pitcher of water and the bowl for washing at
> our bedsides, the supervised Saturday-night bath in the cold
> bathroom, with a red-faced nun sitting on a stool behind a
> drawn curtain with our bath towel in her lap. I felt as though I
> stood on the outskirts and observed the ritual of a cult, a cult of
> fashion and elegance in the sphere of religion.

At the less rarefied end of the spectrum, the lives of teaching
nuns could be chaotic. They had to scramble to prepare for the
courses they were expected to teach (suddenly pursuing a degree
in biology, if the diocese discovered a dearth of science instruc-
tors). They also had to be ready to move at any time to towns and
cities where there were teacher shortages and new schools being
built. As one nun describes it, if an envelope materialized by
your plate at mealtime, you knew you would soon be pulling up

stakes, for inside were the details of your new assignment. In addition, the nuns were confronting startling new issues like delinquency and poverty in their students. After all, most of the nuns hailed from ethnic enclaves and homogeneous, rural places, and came of age in the convent cocoon. It took an open heart and a certain degree of resourcefulness to adapt to their new circumstances with anything approaching grace.

The elderly Sisters of Loretto, whose teaching territories included Kentucky and Texas, well remember that jarring introduction to the real world. "The parents would put their children in Catholic school thinking that because they paid tuition everything would be fine," says Sister Margaret Rose Knoll. "Well, it wasn't fine! We had kids we couldn't handle. We were not prepared." Eventually Sister Margaret Rose must have become acclimated to youth culture, judging from her mastery of the lingo. "This one girl wouldn't let the other children out of the cloakroom—she was terrible," the sister says, in her small, shaky voice. "She was going to rearrange my face on one occasion!" To the sister's relief, the girl was ultimately placed in a school for children with special needs.

Race was also an unfamiliar issue for many of the sisters sent to teach in all-black schools. One elderly Loretto sister betrays her own biases in the manner of someone from another era entirely. "All I saw was this black wall," she admits, remembering the first day of class. "How do you know where one starts and the other one stops?" But by the end of the year, when people would ask her, "You teach in an all-black school, don't you?" she had achieved a considerable degree of sensitivity. "Black, white, pink, gold—I didn't know what they were," the sister says. "They were *children*!" Her eventual enlightenment illustrates another common paradox in the sisters of her era. So many who chose to enter the convent were predisposed to a quiet, controlled life, yet their work often sent them to the front line. The result was a strangely savvy breed of onetime naïfs.

Dedicated as the teaching nuns were, the prevailing preconcilar mind-set held that apostolic work was secondary to the spiritual dimension in the life of a woman religious. The intensive daily upkeep of her relationship with God came first, of course, while the business of teaching, nursing, or working in an orphanage was, for many nuns, merely the dutiful execution of the order's charism—that is, the spirit and the character of the order as envisioned by its foundress. It is surprising to discover how many older nuns had stumbled into the work they did—sometimes wholly unaware, upon entering, of what their order's charism even was. Youthful obliviousness was a factor, but so was the common tendency in those days to focus on the life's more ethereal prospects.

By the mid-twentieth century, the teaching sister was an icon, an object of fascination for daydreaming adolescents who often wondered during class, "What is going *on* under those robes?" However otherworldly they sometimes seemed, the nuns coached field hockey and ice-skated and weren't distracted by a complicated home life from the needs of their students. Given the nuns' effectiveness and dedication, as well as their emphasis on strict discipline, many non-Catholics and even anti-Catholics through the years have sent their children to parochial school in the hope that they would be steeped in excellence and kept out of trouble.

But the tradition of the teaching sister began to wane after Vatican II mandated a reexamination of charisms. Suddenly nuns felt encouraged to exercise social conscience, which meant extending their reach beyond the Catholic classroom. Many communities instituted a policy called "open placement," which for the first time gave sisters a real say in what jobs they could take and where. Other progressive communities allowed a full-scale reinterpretation of their charisms: No longer did "teaching" necessarily mean instructing pupils in a parochial school. Now it might mean teaching English as a second language, training employees in a secular corporation, or counseling teenagers in family planning.

Many sisters were struck by the exhilarating sense of possibility, as they boarded planes in street clothes and embarked on their far-flung assignments. But other sisters lamented the incipient dissolution of the life they had known. Those who had been content to be the religious equivalent of housewives—taking care of the convent and looking after the priests (cooking for them and laundering their vestments)—felt utterly out of step. As enterprising sisters moved away, convent populations started thinning, while laypeople had to be brought in to help maintain the inefficient, expensive manses that had been left behind. Inevitably nuns' ranks in schools and hospitals began to dwindle as well. Even the prestigious Society of the Sacred Heart was not immune to the changes. Between 1968 and 1972 twelve of its thirty-one American schools closed. Perhaps this was to be expected, as the notion of what constituted nuns' work was being thoroughly reconceived.

"I grew up in Ohio, the ninth of ten children," says Sister Marge Eilerman, a Sister of Saint Francis of Tiffin, Ohio. "We were raised very Catholic. In our family it wasn't a matter of whether you were going to church or not, but what Mass do you want to go to? The first Saturday of every month you knew you were going to get carted off to confession, whether you'd sinned or not."

Her father was a farmer who grew corn and oats and raised pigs and chickens. Sister Marge fondly remembers tending the fields with him and cooking and canning with her mother. "We had lots of love, but not lots of things," Sister Marge says in her measured, husky whisper. Even though she attended public school, all but one student in her graduating class of twenty-one were Catholics.

She is sitting at a plywood coffee table in her narrow, one-story home in Booneville, an economically depressed Kentucky backwater with a high rate of illiteracy, where a number of residents depend on marijuana crops for survival. There are large, framed photographs of Mexican women and children on the wall, along with a wooden cross several feet high. It is left over from the days when people celebrated Mass here in Sister Marge's living room; every night the furniture had to be moved into the kitchen beforehand. Finally, in 1991, a log cabin–style church that Sister Marge helped design was built for the county's Catholic community, which currently numbers about sixteen families—the clear minority in this heavily Baptist and fundamentalist region. (When Sister Marge first arrived in 1984, the Catholic population stood at about one.) As she talks, a lawnmower drones and hummingbirds vibrate around the feeder hanging by the front door.

At sixty years old Sister Marge has snowy curls, tinted eyeglasses, and soft, grandmotherly contours beneath her sporty red polo shirt and khakis. She also wears running shoes with a University of Kentucky wildcat on the tongue, in cheerful solidarity with her neighbors, ardent college basketball fans all. As she shares sepia-toned memories of her innocent, churchgoing background and her straightforward path to the convent, Sister Marge sounds like a textbook example of a pre–Vatican II woman religious—not the prison-bound felon that she is.

Sister Marge isn't the only nun whose life ended up on side roads and detours that she never could have imagined when she took the veil all those decades ago. Despite her limited exposure to nuns as a child (back then if a girl didn't attend Catholic school, chances are she didn't know any nuns), Sister Marge was drawn to the idea of religious life. "It was a dream," she says. "Something that spoke to my heart, even though I didn't know what it meant." Somewhat less mystically, her parents had plenty of other children, so she knew they would be okay without her. She also loved the idea of the habit—"I just thought that would be so cool to wear." Then one day the dream actually seemed attainable. When Sister Marge went to visit her cousin in a Franciscan community, she felt as if she'd come home. "It was cheerful," she says. "There was a group of sisters sitting in a circle peeling peaches, having what they called a peach party. There was a warmth, there was a joy. It was very clear that this is what I wanted to do." Sometime later, after a special dinner of ham and tomatoes stuffed with egg salad at her sister's, Marge went to the convent. For that momentous trip she was wearing a red dress, of all things—a last gasp of brazen secularism. But almost immediately upon her arrival at the convent, she had to change into the black clothes her mother had made for her. It was 1957. She was twenty years old.

Sister Marge's years in the novitiate were difficult, and not so much because the women were living ten or twelve to a room, with drapes hanging from a pipe that served as a wall between each of their cells. It was the long list of seemingly meaningless rules that she didn't appreciate, like not being allowed to dine with visitors, pose for family photographs, write or receive letters, or read the newspaper. Nor was she enthusiastic about the teaching career she seemed destined for, once she had taken her final vows. By the late sixties, however, new opportunities were brewing. Along with modifying the habit, the community, like so many others, was discussing the possibility of different kinds of work among the poor, in inner cities and other countries. During one such meeting, Sister Marge remembers, "One of my friends and I were crying. We were just so intent that it was time to break out of the mold. So our mother superior said, 'Okay, if we're going to do this, if we're going to allow people to go'—to exotic, troubled places—'then I need to know who is willing.' " With very little hesitation Sister Marge volunteered. In a matter of months she boarded an airplane for the first time in her life and flew to Mexico, to the rugged, sparsely populated state of Chiapas, with its jungle vegetation and ominous military presence.

Everything about this kind of missionary work felt right to her. Providing support for the peasants, talking about Scripture, teaching women about hygiene and self-respect, Sister Marge also developed an understanding of Latin American politics, and the role of the United States in perpetuating violence there. Her time in Chiapas would set the stage for what would become her real calling: the vigorous and sustained protest of the School of the Americas, a United States–funded military program at Fort Benning, Georgia, that trains Latin American soldiers in paramilitary skills and strategies, including torture techniques. Graduates, who include former Panamanian dictator Manuel Noriega and Salvadoran death-squad organizer Roberto D'Aubuisson, have been linked to a number of human-rights atrocities, including the 1980 murder in El Salvador of three Catholic sisters and a laywoman, and the 1989 murder in El Salvador of two women and six Jesuit priests, one of whose brains were scooped from his skull and tossed on the ground. As Sister Marge would often put it, she "wanted to do something big for God." Protesting these kinds of atrocities was it.

In 1996 Sister Marge began participating in prayer vigils and eventually protests, replete with macabre street theater, effigies, crosses, and the symbolic digging of graves—at the Pentagon as well as at Fort Benning. Police were involved and arrests were sometimes made, but it was an incident in November 1997 that would finally land Sister Marge in prison. The action involved altering the austere sign at the entrance to the compound that read WELCOME TO FORT BENNING U.S. ARMY MILITARY RESERVATION. By removing some of the metal letters and making new ones with the aid of stencils that the activists had brought along, they changed the sign to read, WELCOME TO FORT BENNING: HOME OF SCHOOL OF AMERICAS, SCHOOL OF SHAME, SOA=TORTURE. Bloody handprints and smears would then be applied to the sign using some of the protesters' blood mixed with a red oxide.

Sister Marge's job was to pry off the letters using a crowbar. "I remember the elation of that," she says. "We didn't know if they'd come off, and when they did, I remember saying, 'They come off! They come off!' When we were finished, we stacked up the letters and made it look neat and orderly." The old-school nun in her rearing up? Not really. "We were careful not to do anything that would cause anyone to draw a gun on you or your fellow activists."

As she tells her story, it is interesting to see Sister Marge's level of intensity and interest deepen the moment she starts talking about the protests. She leans in close and her tone grows conspiratorial, while her attention to detail and her recall seem to increase. You can almost see the goose bumps rising on her skin. Especially when she gets to the part where she finally is arrested—this time for a felony: the malicious destruction of government property. The shamed demeanor of the female officer who had to arrest her, the surreality of being handcuffed behind her back, the way the metal cuffs pinched and chafed, the officer making sure that Marge didn't bump her head as she guided her into the backseat of the squad car—Sister Marge has clearly replayed these details over and over in her mind many times since. "My sense of being arrested as an innocent person," she says, "filled me with the feeling of being one with Jesus."

In two separate trials Sister Marge was convicted of trespassing and the destruction of government property. Unfortunately for her, the judge she and her fellow activists faced was the conservative, then-eighty-nine-year-old J. Robert "Maximum Bob" Elliott, notable for having once denied Martin Luther King, Jr., the right to march, and for attempting to reverse the decision against Lt. William Calley for his role in the My Lai massacre. It wasn't a surprise that the plight of the Fort Benning protesters failed to move him. All told, the judge sentenced Sister Marge to $4,050 in fines and restitution and fourteen months in prison.

In a matter of weeks Sister Marge will begin her sentence in Atwood Prison in Lexington, Kentucky, where she will share a room with eleven other women, most of whom have committed either drug crimes or money-related offenses like embezzlement. The only personal items she will be allowed to take are prescription eyeglasses and the silver ring signifying her status as a Franciscan. Her well-worn Bible has to remain at home. But nothing about this frightens her. As a nun she knows about hard work and stripped-down surroundings—she has already lived in a cell during her years in the convent. "Prison doesn't hold the fear for me that it might for some people, because I have been out there alone," she says. This is simply the next page in the most invigorating chapter of her life.

Sister Marge pulls out a meticulously maintained scrapbook devoted to the protests: itineraries, newspaper clippings, official summonses, and violation notices, along with the envelopes they came in; the words "The truth cannot be silenced" on a purple backing that had been trimmed with pinking shears; a stone in an evidence bag that was retrieved by the authorities from a mass grave dug by the protesters in front of the Pentagon. This stone is Sister Marge's prized possession; she says she wants to be buried with it.

But the most telling artifacts are the photographs showing Sister Marge getting ready with the other activists, smiling behind sunglasses, looking fierce. If she were an athlete, one might say she has her game face on. Judging from the photographs, it is clear that this is what she was called to do, even though her family had to joke that she'd got it all mixed up: Getting arrested at protests is what people did in *the* sixties, not in *their* sixties.

So then what of the peach party and the floor-length habit Sister Marge had once thought would be "so cool" to wear? Amazingly, much of that small-town Catholic is still in her.

Disdainful as they are of authoritarian models of any kind, so many active, political post–Vatican II sisters have strayed from the church's compulsory rituals, neglecting to attend a formal Mass for long stretches of time. But Sister Marge's devotion to the transporting rites runs deep. Despite her proclivity for insurrection, she is humbled by the glorious tradition of church. In fact, she laments the degree to which some of the Booneville parishioners are "unchurched": Converts to the faith, they weren't inculcated in childhood with the stories and traditions that root the Catholic and function as a lifeline in hard times.

In Booneville, with daylight splintering in the trees before Mass, death squads and urgent bills before Congress seem worlds away. A local family of seven files into the log-cabin church, taking their regular seats in the front pew. The young man suffering from a muscle disease glides through in his wheelchair. The middle-aged good neighbor arrives with a squash from her garden—a gift for another parishioner. Father Richard comes in with a few worshippers who needed a ride. Perhaps there are thirty people in all. During the kiss of peace everyone has a chance to embrace everyone else.

When it is time for the offertory, Sister Marge moves toward a small table to retrieve the wine and wafers. The wine is contained in a cut-glass cruet, and the wafers sit on a clay plate. She brings both to Father Richard, who is wearing a white ecclesiastical robe called an alb. After consecrating the wine and wafers, he distributes them to the congregation with Sister Marge's assistance. Enveloped in a sense of belonging and hopefulness, renewed by the regular miracle of Eucharist, the parishioners return to the pews. After Mass they will all go to the Fellowship Hall next door for coffee, cake, and cookies.

On the face of it there is an obvious conflict between the daily demands of a grassroots ministry and the extraordinary exertions of political activism. But Sister Marge doesn't see it that way. At Fort Benning she was crusading for social justice, and that is what she has done in Booneville. Advocating for neighbors in trouble, hosting groups in which women who might be destitute or abused can finally express themselves, Sister Marge has consistently been committed to organizing the disenfranchised and giving them a voice.

But being there for a neighbor who needs a ride to the hospital and being available for jail time ultimately don't mix. When she has completed her sentence in Atwood, Sister Marge won't return to Booneville. Instead she will move back to Ohio and devote herself full-time to the cause, disseminating information about the School of the Americas. She has no doubt now: This is the work she was called to do.

Today many nuns find themselves searching for a balance between religious tradition and the glaringly modern cast of their vocation, along with the style of life it requires. Sometimes the two seem almost irreconcilable. For a time I volunteered at an AIDS hospice in New York City that was run by the Missionaries of Charity—the order founded by Mother Teresa of Calcutta. Quietly industrious and demure in their white cotton robes and sandals, the nuns were a clear joy to the hard-edged male patients they tended to so cheerfully ("You got a carton of smokes under there for me, Sister?" one of the patients liked to say, with a flirtatious glance at a nun's robes). One day, having wiped down the plastic-sheathed mattresses with ammonia, I was in the kitchen chopping vegetables for soup when the superior came in. She asked me if I'd accompany one of their young nuns to a nearby hospital where she was to receive a dialysis treatment. Moments later we boarded the Ambulette outside, the young nun careful to pull in the edges of her habit before the driver slid the door shut.

She was a frail twenty-eight-year-old with large, delicate eyes, who'd come from India to work in shelters and soup kitchens in the Bronx, Harlem, and now Greenwich Village. She was so small and soft-spoken, it was amazing to think of her pursuing such a grueling path in life. When we reached the hospital, I wished her good luck, but the nun made it clear she wanted me to take her inside. It seemed a little strange: Although her kidneys were apparently malfunctioning, she had no trouble negotiating streets or stairs. It was only once we had reached the dialysis unit that I felt she was okay with my leaving.

Back at the hospice another volunteer cleared up the mystery: It wasn't physical support the nun needed from me. In her order, the nuns are forbidden from traveling any distance alone. They can feed the poor in dangerous, faraway neighborhoods, they can save lives and comfort the dying on a daily basis, but they aren't allowed to walk around Greenwich Village by themselves. To me this seemed an excruciating paradox.

Many contemporary sisters are immune to such paradoxes because they are living very much on their own. Any number of forces, including the changing nature of their work, spun them out of the convents, requiring them to rethink their place in the world. But there is also a sense in which the modern nun is returning to a seminal form of religious life.

In the first half of this century nuns were deployed like troops to hospitals and schools. Their modus operandi had grown so effective and time-tested that their mission had assumed a distinctly corporate cast. This was a far cry from the renegade spirit of the fervent fourth-century religious women whose love of God drove them into a state of prayerful solitude in the desert. Emboldened by Vatican II, some nuns saw an opportunity to return to those ancestral ideals. One sister, whose work in a homeless shelter leaves no time for Mass or regular rounds of prayer, sees nothing incongruous in a life that is both unstructured and vowed. "I think this is the kind of work Jesus would be doing if He were here now," the sister says.

The simple truth of that sentiment is easily forgotten in an institution as wealthy and hierarchical as the Catholic Church. In *Guests in Their Own House*, by Carmel McEnroy, one female auditor of Vatican II recalls the air of opulence and pomp that accompanied the cardinals who came to the council in rustling silks, attended by chauffeurs or bodyguards:

> They usually arrived in very impressive black Cadillacs, or limousines like those certain U.S. presidents used. The license plates were engraved with the letters SCV (which means *Sacra Citta Vaticana*), but there were jokes about what it *really* meant. The Italians said it stood for *Se Cristo Vedesse* (if Christ could see) the luxury that surrounded these representatives of the church he founded.

The modern Church is also saddled with a bureaucracy that is arguably at odds with what Christ had in mind. The ceaseless councils, committees, subcommittees, and conferences that seem better suited to a multinational corporation might be unavoidable in such a vast and many-tentacled organization. But it is somehow not surprising to learn that a great many nuns, disinterested in the politics, slipped the structure when they saw the chance. One woman grew so disillusioned in her increasingly corporate, heavily administrated order, she had no choice but to leave religious life altogether. "Our founder wanted us to carry the soup kettle," she says, "not give a hundred dollars to the soup kitchen down the street." Still other similarly disenchanted sisters attempted to refashion religious life itself.

"I wanted to live more counterculturally," says Sister Nancy Chiarello of her predictable nursing tour during her early years as a Franciscan Sister of Allegany, New York. At the time she was living in institutional quarters located above the hospital. Eventually she and three other sisters got permission from the mother superior to move in together in New York City. Her life changed the day one of her roommates saw a woman eating out of a garbage can. "A lightbulb went on," Sister Nancy says. "Why are women eating out of garbage cans in this day and age?" Once she began to investigate the situation, it shocked her to realize that sexism existed on virtually every level of society: Even destitute men had access to facilities and programs that hadn't even been conceived of for women. She and her sisters were determined to do something about that. With the help of the diocese, they bought a four-story walk-up on a rough block just west of the Port Authority bus terminal, where blood trickles down the sidewalk from the fish store on the corner. But it is home. Called the Dwelling Place, the shelter is an exemplary product of Vatican II thinking, in that the sisters identified a contemporary problem and addressed it with age-old spirituality. The Dwelling Place presaged a post–Vatican II trend in women taking care of women.

At first, the sisters' dreams collided with the harshest realities. When the crack epidemic hit in the early eighties, they were policing dinner crowds of up to two hundred (the dining room is better suited to about eighty diners a night). Being bitten and punched by the desperate and drug-addled was a common hazard of the job, although many of the most disruptive women fell away when Sister Nancy raised the minimum age to thirty. Now, twenty-two years after it opened its doors, the Dwelling Place is a much more orderly, even homey, affair. Its purpose is to give women a haven where they can live for a while, pull themselves together, and get referrals for apartments and jobs. It is also a place where they can feel respected and cared for before heading back into the world. A psychiatrist and a physician's assistant come by regularly to provide services.

On my first visit to the Dwelling Place in 1995, I was put to work before Sister Justine Nutz even learned my name. Silently, side by side, we hauled huge boxes of beef patties and apricots and bags of corn into the massive freezer in the storage room that doubles as a clinic (the nuns simply drape sheets over the canned goods and boxes when the volunteer medical team comes by to conduct physicals).

Later Sister Justine and I were in the small office upstairs when a jittery young woman appeared, all made up and dressed for a weekend in Baltimore. "Kiss the ground when you get there," Sister Justine said. "I do love that town." Then she asked the girl to hand over the bottle of pills the sister knew she had with her (the sisters dispense medications and carefully monitor the women's intake). Sister Justine asked how many pills the woman had taken. Seven, she said, which meant there should be fifty-three left in the bottle. As the woman prepared to go, Sister Justine quickly started to count the remaining pills, when suddenly we heard screams from downstairs.

A frantic phone call came from the shelter's octogenarian cook, asking Sister Justine to come down right away. Apparently someone who had been banned from the shelter that morning for making trouble was back and was shoving the cook trying to gain entrance. As she ran for the stairs, Sister Justine thrust the bottle of pills at me and said, "You count." I came up with fifty-two, my hands shaking as I did, while Sister Justine attempted to contain the hysterical woman downstairs until the police arrived. This was business as usual at the Dwelling Place. "We call it the

Ministry of Interruptions," Sister Justine said upon her return, with an exhausted laugh.

Does it matter if a nun's work effectively keeps her from church and convent life? Is she somehow less a nun if her prayer takes place in a corner room on the upper floor of a tenement building in midtown, her conversations with God punctuated by buses and trucks belching exhaust? Despite some crosses here and there, the Dwelling Place doesn't look like the holiest place in New York. The women in residence aren't even expected to visit the chapel (Sister Nancy disapproves of charitable organizations that barter with food: We'll give you a meal if you pray with us first). But if holiness means living as Jesus did by loving and serving the poor, then the Dwelling Place is the Vatican of the street. The nuns' work includes counseling the homeless women, feeding and hugging them, following up on their job and apartment prospects, reminding them to take their medicine, throwing Halloween and Christmas parties for them, and patting their pregnant stomachs.

Despite the nuns' earthy accessibility, however, they maintain a vigilant respect for their purpose. That was apparent during a planning meeting for the shelter's twentieth anniversary. Always worried about operational costs, the sisters expressed a desire to attract some kind of attention to the event, perhaps by turning it into a benefit. So the media-savvy minds of some volunteers started to race—how about inviting Mayor Rudolph Giuliani, who's always eager for a photo op? But the nuns weren't interested. They would rather struggle than taint the spirit of their gathering with the sort of strategic cynicism that makes the worlds of politics and the media go round. While their spirituality keeps them from being as practical as they might be, it is also what makes them nuns.

Sister Nancy lives at the Dwelling Place, up a few steep flights of stairs from the kitchen and dining room. Her spartan quarters vibrate with traffic noise. The only visible concessions to comfort are a television and two recliners.

Sister Nancy doesn't look or sound like the stereotypical nun. Built round and strong, with red-framed glasses and large brown puppy eyes, she's a kidder and a laugher. Yet she also talks in tough, New York–y cadences that suggest a bone-deep disinclination to be messed with (fittingly, perhaps, for the daughter of the onetime fillet man down at the Fulton Fish Market). When tempers flare among the homeless women, she and a few of the other take-charge nuns move forcefully into the dining room, arms bowed as they circle the tables slowly, restoring order with their powerful presence (altogether there are six nuns at the shelter). Sister Nancy tells nun jokes and swears; she once described the decision of whether or not to enter religious life as being a matter of "shit or get off the pot." She wears jeans and flannel shirts, often with a pack of cigarettes tucked in the breast pocket. One of the first times I came to see Sister Nancy, she had just taken a phone call from a refrigerator repairman. "I'm fine," she was saying, with a cigarette clenched between her teeth. "How the hell are you?" She drinks wine and plays motorboat with little kids in her sister's pool on Staten Island. (In the old days not only did you never see a nun eat, you absolutely never saw her in a bathing suit.) Hanging on her bathroom wall is a poster called "Religious Views of Life":

Taoism: Shit Happens.
Judaism: Why does this shit always happen to us?
Agnosticism: What is this shit?
Atheism: I don't believe this shit.
Catholicism: If shit happens, you deserve it.

"I remember questioning a lot of things when I was growing up," she says. "Things that just didn't make sense. As a kid I couldn't understand why if a baby died and hadn't been baptized, it was going to Limbo"—as stipulated in the Baltimore Catechism, the Catholic's pre–Vatican II religious instruction manual. "That baby didn't do anything! I couldn't believe that God would allow that. I just couldn't buy into it. And the question of whether the Blessed Mother was a virgin when she conceived is so mundane. That's not the key to salvation. But to capture the spirit of how she lived her life on earth as a follower, the bearer of Jesus!" That, for Sister Nancy, has some meaning.

The more strident teachings of the institutional church are a waste of time to nuns like Sister Nancy, whose immersion in life-or-death ministries has turned them into outspoken realists. She flatly admits that Rome just isn't a factor in her life. She thinks about the pope only to the extent that he disappoints her, by not listening to women religious, by silencing freethinking theologians, and by refusing to engage in the political situations that oppress the poor here and in Third World countries. When Vatican II "hit the fan," as Sister Nancy puts it, nuns finally started thinking for themselves and doing work that responded to the way we live now. As for the trappings, like the habit, that fell away, Sister Nancy says good riddance. "People think, 'This is what nuns should be. Why aren't you in habit?' And I say, 'Does that change who I am, what I do, what I believe?' If it does, then that's the sin."

In the broad variety of nuns' work and its purpose, there is a critical distinction between being and doing. For Sister Margaret Traxler grace is in the doing. "They always say it is what you are that matters, and your union with God will determine the fruits of your labors," she says, "because it is God who gives the increase. Not I. I have this feeling that whatever I do, I must do it well"—which in her case has meant advocating relentlessly for women, prisoners, and the poor.

In a sense the central question of the habit applies in the realm of nuns' work: Whom is it for? Is it a highly personal expression of one's faith or is it a means of extending oneself into the world? Those nuns who subscribe to the former interpretation couldn't help but resent the "anything goes" mentality that seemed to be creeping in with Vatican II.

"My feeling is that when Vatican II came in, too many orders threw out the baby with the bathwater," says Mother Hildegard, who is mystified by the urban apostolic frenzy of the last thirty years. "I have nothing against people doing things in the inner city. Our Lord says, 'The poor are always with you,' and I'm not saying we shouldn't be out there helping them. But what happened was that so many of the orders just closed the doors of their schools and said, 'We've got to go out there and be one with the people.' Well, I don't think it has worked. They might be doing good work, but the people don't respect them in the same way. And we've certainly lost the kids. My feeling is that the religious in this country did a great disservice to the church by giving up the schools. You give up the schools, you've lost the vocations. Because that's where the vocations come from."

None of this much applies to Mother Hildegard. As a contemplative, full-time teaching was never an option for her. Although she does teach catechism, Mother Hildegard's work is focused largely on farming. Along with raising animals for wool and meat, her community runs the last hand dairy in existence in

Washington State. Naturally the inspectors—"all these young whippersnappers right out of university"—can be a nuisance. "Now everything has to be covered in plastic. And whenever there's an *E. coli* outbreak, they come right to us."

On a brisk March day, wearing a black sweatshirt over her habit and a blue knit cap pulled tight over her veil, Mother Hildegard feeds the llamas, whose long ears hitch forward when they see her. Approaching their pen, she trills their names in a theatrical falsetto—"La Morenita!" which means the "little black-faced one." "Come here to Mother," she says, putting the llama in a headlock and taking a blade of grass out of her eye. She named another llama El Dorado, on account of the money the nuns hope to make when they sell him. El Dorado cocks his rear end at Mother Hildegard, as if he is posing. "Look at him! He's just so pizzazzy! He's just *got* it!" she says, her habit riding up as she reaches for a bale of hay, revealing a pair of black nylon knee-highs underneath. Then she lowers the bale onto her shoulder and heaves it into the pen. Elsewhere the convent cat is picking its way gingerly through the grass, its meow sounding like a rusty hinge as a result of having its throat slashed a few Halloweens ago, before being taken in by the nuns.

Over in the sheep meadow a tiny white lamb only fifteen days old comes tumbling and bleating after Mother Hildegard. Born with pinkeye, he was rejected by his mother, so Mother Hildegard had to bottle-feed him. She picks up the lamb and kisses his face and neck. He collapses into her chest affectionately. They look like an Easter card.

If at all possible, Mother Hildegard likes to avoid bottle-feeding; "they're brats when they're bottle-fed, and it's a lot of work," she points out. She has her ways. "In a big flock you might have a baby orphaned the same day a mother loses her lamb, and you would want to put the orphan together with her," Mother Hildegard says, and explains how this might be accomplished: "You could skin the dead lamb and then lay the skin over the orphan, so the mother will smell it thinking it's hers. That's one way. Another way is to spray something on the mother's nose, then on the baby, especially its rear end because that's the first place the mother smells. Some people use vanilla; I always use White Shoulders. The third thing, the desperate thing, is to tie the mother up for a couple of days in a pen and let the baby keep nursing." Mother Hildegard, who is well educated and shrewd, has been at this a long time. Even now she and Mother Prioress ride the ferry to the mainland once a week to take a livestock course that will qualify them as experts. On a recent morning Mother Prioress, who had fallen behind in her studies, was filling out her "chicken test" on the ferry while consulting a textbook called *Your Chickens*.

After the animals are fed, the nuns eat their midday meal—meat loaf from the meat of a bull who'd broken its leg. Then Mother Hildegard makes marmalade. In the canning room, anchored by a stainless-steel table and huge sinks, she retrieves some chopped kumquats from the walk-in refrigerator and puts them in a pot on the stove. She adds sugar and cooks down the mixture, eventually dipping in a spoon and inspecting it, checking for "sheeting" and then "balling." One wants the consistency to be thick enough that the drips drop like balls into the pot. Then she boils mason jars and lids, pulls them out with tongs, and fills them with marmalade.

Elsewhere, Mother Felicitas is making potpourri. Mother Felicitas is a divorced mother of two grown sons who still remembers the joy of those "little fetal pokes" during pregnancy. Many communities won't even allow such a person to enter, but Mother Felicitas was in many ways a good fit. She has a doctorate in musicology and lends much to the considerable portions of the day that are consumed by chanting. She says the music is what drew her to the monastery in the first place. That and the need to do something special with her life once her marriage fell apart. "I remember reading an article about someone in his thirties running an African country," she says. "And I thought, 'Gee, he's doing that, and what have I done?' "

In gold-rimmed bifocals, a white knit cap, and a black windbreaker worn over her habit, Mother Felicitas brings a large box of lavender in from the herb garden. Then she starts rubbing the little purple buds off the stalks into a bucket. At a certain point, when the lavender starts to make Mother Felicitas's eyes and nose itch, she ties a red bandanna around her face, making her look hilariously like a bank-robbing nun.

The potpourri will be for sale, as will the marmalade and wool. In the past Mother Hildegard even made soaps and perfumes and sold them at abbey fairs. To a large extent this hard work is about subsistence. A few years ago, at the community's sprawling abbey in Connecticut, the nuns ingeniously managed to replenish their coffers by capitalizing on lay interest in Gregorian chant. They recorded a CD that wound up selling well. Whatever works: Contemplative nuns live every day with a certain degree of financial anxiety.

But the hard work is also about preserving their independence and their separateness from the rest of the world. Self-sustaining labors give them a safe space for contemplation and prayer, while contemplation and prayer burnish their labors. "St. Benedict tried to find the Spirit in everything that he did," Mother Hildegard says. "One of my favorite sayings of his is 'Treat everything like sacred vessels of the altar.' I don't care if it's the hay you're throwing in the pile or the dishes you're drying. You should treat everything with respect. He just had an ethic of taking pleasure and pride in work, seeing that it was a gift from God. And we've certainly lost that in our modern society. How many people really love their work?"

Despite the backbreaking nature of agrarian life, it has an obvious appeal. Amid the earthy smells and the sound of cowbells and crowing roosters, one can easily appreciate its hypnotic routines and soothing rhythms. As one former Trappistine described her years on the farm, "It was water, it was steel buckets, it was being with creatures, like being with children: warm breath and smelly bottoms, birth and death—it was beautiful. Those days in the barn were some of the happiest days of my life."

Back when nuns' ranks were flush, it was easier for them to be open-minded about the variety of ways one might live a religious life. Only now that their future is in question are some nuns scrutinizing the way other nuns do things, as if the choices of one undermine those of another. Clearly some contemplative nuns think that holding jobs in the lay world is the slippery slope to secularization. The skepticism goes both ways. In a conversation about the contemplative agrarian life, one fiercely apostolic, shelter-founding sister snorted, "Feeding cows is fine, but what about feeding the poor?"

The circumstances and cultural realities of time and place surely influence the work that nuns do. The demand for homeless shelters for women was negligible in the fifties compared to what it became in the eighties. Similarly, the importance of being bilingual is greater in a Texas border town than it is in Wisconsin, and so on. For active sisters especially, the nature of the work is always evolving. Which raises the question, What in a nun's life, if anything, is fixed?

EVERY NOOK AND CRANNY

OF MY SOUL

The Prayer Life

❖

P ERHAPS THE MOST MYSTIFYING
aspect of religious life is the relationship with God that lives at its
center. The liturgy is full of pleading requests to God to become
visible and allow Himself to be known: "Your face, Lord, do I
seek. Do not hide Your face from me." (Ps. 27:8–9); "Let the light
of Your face shine on us, O Lord!" (Ps. 4:6); "My soul thirsts for
God, the living God. When shall I come and behold the face of
God?" (Ps. 42:2). Judging from Scripture, and from some nuns'
chronic feelings of doubt and abandonment over the course of a
life spent grasping at the invisible, the Divine can be frustratingly
elusive. But true believers persevere through the fevered enter-

prise called prayer—the sister's dogged daily ritual of reaching out and attempting to communicate with her inscrutable beloved.

In a very real sense communicating with God is the nun's life-work, which explains most nuns' capacity for prompt and polite disengagement from laypeople. Solicitous as they can sometimes be, when their worldly business with you is done, it is done. In most cases a subtle distancing immediately follows, in much the same way a monogamous married person gently moves away from someone he or she is attracted to. For the nun's heart belongs to another, and her real life lies elsewhere—a fact that seems to hover around her.

The idea of a consecrated life of prayer, in which people eschewed the confines of society and matrimony in favor of an exclusive relationship with God, has its roots in the earliest days of the Roman Empire. At the time a woman's options were narrow and few. The Augustan marriage laws rewarded those who wed and produced three children—braving the constant threat of death by childbirth, while those who did not were seen as social failures and essentially treated as children themselves. Still, some defiantly embraced a life of celibacy, while others pursued even more radical alternatives.

A direct ancestral line can be drawn between contemporary religious and the desert mothers and fathers of the fourth century. Women and men of the day, desirous of a total communion with God, frequently fled the city for the desert—"the wild place without limit or definition, which represented withdrawal from worldly entanglement, purification, and contact with the divine," as Jo Ann McNamara writes in *Sisters in Arms*. Here one could confront oneself as well as God in the stark asceticism of a primitive life. Such an existence was unimaginably difficult, often including extended periods of fasting, but its challenges were also its gifts. The desert mothers and fathers pioneered the tradition of atonement and transcendence through discipline and self-denial that is still operating in monasteries sixteen centuries later.

The template of monasticism took shape in the fourth, fifth, and sixth centuries as newly forming ascetic communities began congregating for communal worship. Eventually a daily regimen of Scripture read aloud and prayerful song chanted in unison became the prescribed mode of Christian prayer known as the Divine Office. It was and remains a cornerstone of monastic life, giving shape to the day much as the four seasons contour the year. Like winter giving way to spring, the quiet chill of nightly matins leads to the robust morning energy of lauds, while the twilight of vespers dissolves into the somber finality of compline.

In addition to providing a liturgical link to the past, the Divine Office—or the Liturgy of the Hours, as it became known after Vatican II—is effective in keeping the nun focused on the heavy task at hand: the continual upkeep of her relationship with God. When one is due in chapel seven times a day, there is barely enough time for chores, which are endless in a rambling monastery, and opportunities for distracting and unholy leisure are almost nonexistent. Commitment to a life spent within the cloister seems reasonable in light of the demanding prayer schedule, as even some of one's free periods are expected to be used for prayer. Quite simply, there isn't time for much of anything besides God.

That said, the degree of faith and fervor required by such a life is unfathomable.

* * *

At 7:15 A.M. on a still March day, some sixteen nuns file into the chapel for morning prayer (when all are present, the community numbers nineteen). Except for the two postulants who are still in secular clothes, each is wearing a wooden cross pendant over a shapeless, knee-length tan dress cinched at the waist with a cord. In the cord are four knots, signifying the nuns' vows of poverty, chastity, obedience, and enclosure.

These are the Poor Clares of Greenville, South Carolina. The Poor Clares are a cloistered contemplative order founded by St. Clare of Assisi, the thirteenth-century follower of St. Francis whose devotion to the "poor Christ" entailed a kind of "interior poverty"—an emptying out and ridding oneself of impediments like falseness and ego. It also involved a total renunciation of all possessions and human comforts—that is, anything that could conceivably come between her and Christ, including footwear and beds. In addition, Clare insisted that those who followed her could never receive or own property of any kind. To say the least, she was a purist. So severe was her vision that when it came time for Pope Innocent III to ratify her rule, Clare had to beg him for the "privilege of poverty." While many of her contemporary followers have adapted the tenets somewhat, allowing shoes in some communities after centuries of orthopedic miseries, they talk with great fondness and familiarity about Clare; honoring her vision through the humble and prayerful observance of her spirit is a driving force of their lives.

Despite the odd flash of individuality—a blue cardigan here, interesting sandals there—the women in this Poor Clare community are bonded by a surface uniformity. While the wearing of a short, neat haircut and eyeglasses is not mandated in the order's constitution, it is the inevitable, low-maintenance look of a woman who doesn't get out much. Every sister is also wearing a wristwatch, with good reason: Adhering to a strict prayer schedule that stretches over the course of the entire day, she must not be late to the chapel. In that sense the women's outer uniformity is reflective of a much deeper one.

The nuns take their assigned seats in the two sets of choir stalls facing one another and settle in for some deep contemplation together, alone. Several of the women are angled toward the front of the choir, staring at the tabernacle that houses the "body of Christ." Befitting the discreet, modest character of the sisters, the tabernacle is a simple, spotlit box that looks like a Danish Modern humidor, with doors that are opened—a far cry from the gaudy, curtained, gilt affairs that flourished before Vatican II. Resting outside the box is a monstrance, a kind of pedestal holding a consecrated wafer that Catholics believe to be the Real Presence of Christ's body. Many nuns find the tabernacle and its contents a useful point of focus during solitary prayer—for some it has attained an almost fetishistic significance—while others prefer to stare up, down, or into the middle distance. Hectic birdsong in the trees beyond the windows, a whirring ceiling fan, and the occasional cough are the only noises in the room.

After several minutes solitary contemplation gives way to choral prayer, in which the nuns on one side of the choir say a few lines of a psalm, followed by a few lines from the nuns on the other side. Today they work with Psalm 119:

> *All that I am longs for You*
> *I wait for Your word.*

My eyes are strained from searching.
When will You comfort me?
Though dried up like old leather
I never forget Your commands
How many days do I have left?

At a certain point one of the nuns begins to read out loud when it is not her turn. It leaves her flustered and abashed, which somehow seems odd. If one cannot make a mistake here, in this closed and tightly knit, familial community, then where? But standards and expectations are heightened beneath the invisible dome of prayer that contains the group. While it may look as if they are among friends, there is Another in their midst. One senses the nervous air of performance for a Divine audience of one.

The sisters say the Lord's Prayer with arms outstretched, palms up.

Worship ends with the doxology—a short and pointed ancient prayer extolling God's eternal majesty—spoken in grim unison:

Glory to the Father, and to the Son, and to the Holy Spirit.
As it was in the beginning, is now and will be forever.
Amen.

Then the sisters slip out of their choir stalls and bend reverently at the waist in the direction of the tabernacle before peeling off left and right, to the twisting halls one level down where each has a room—its door consisting of a small sheet of pretty material hanging on a curtain rod. Their monastery, which is boxy, brick, and institutional, is as deceptively ordinary-looking as the women themselves. There is no stray or superfluous decoration; everything seems stripped down to its essence. And there is no smiling or talking as the women retreat. All seem to maintain "custody of the eyes," that pre–Vatican II custom intended to block out distraction and preserve single-mindedness. Only here it seems less mandated than absolutely natural among women who have God on their minds. If the sisters are fulfilling their vocations as true contemplatives, there is no conceivable need to throw curious glances about. It is interesting that in a community whose members are more inclined to see with their hearts than their eyes, as many as three have seriously impaired vision. Two of the women are nearly blind, while a third, who was born without an eye, wears a glass one.

The women will meet again for more prayer in a couple of hours. And a couple of hours after that, and also after that, seven times a day, for the rest of their lives.

For those of us who wake up with barely enough time to dress and drink coffee while a half dozen worries and plans vie for consideration as we fly out the door, it is difficult to comprehend the intensity of the cloistered life. To begin with, there is no flying out the door: The women are expected to spend almost all of their time within the enclosure, and they are very careful about whom they let in. "You don't just invite anyone inside your enclosure," one sister says. "We don't have an option of going anywhere else—this is where we live. So whomever we bring in is going to influence and touch everyone here."

Strict as that sounds, another sister is quick to say that their daily life isn't anything like prison. They are here by choice and happy for the boundaries that ensure their existence. Besides, unlike in the pre–Vatican II days, when some cloistered nuns spent their lives behind a double layer of iron grates affixed with six-inch metal spikes, these Poor Clares are allowed occasional interaction with laypeople. When some Boy Scouts came to rake leaves on a recent February morning, one sister offered them encouragement and refreshments; she also chatted with work-men who were building a wheelchair ramp for the monastery and negotiated with a computer repairman. The nuns are allowed to pop out for things like doctor and dentist appoint-ments, now and then. But the reasons for popping out really do have to be good ones. "For instance, I'd never just go and hang out at a McDonald's," one sister says.

The idea of enclosure is both practical and philosophical. On a practical level, given that they honor the vow of poverty, the sis-ters wouldn't get very far out in the world without any money. The monastery allots small sums for expenses like doctor bills and new shoes; that money comes from benefactors, as well as from the monastery's various revenue-producing ventures, like the selling of prayer cards and the distribution of altar breads. Like all communities of vowed Catholic women, the Poor Clares have had to be resourceful: It is a widespread misconception that convents and monasteries are supported financially by the dio-cese.

On a philosophical level, enclosure sharpens one's focus on the mission. As the Poor Clares would have it, they are enclosed "for the sake of being opened still more radically to God and to all God's people in world and church." Enclosure blocks out dis-tractions and enhances community. When nineteen women live and work together year after year, they begin to function as a cohesive, organic entity, with all parts pulling together for a common purpose, wordlessly observing common values, like silence. In this community, for instance, it is understood that dinner is a time for lighthearted conversation, while the doing of dishes moments later is not. Almost as in choir, the voices rise and join together during the meal, then dwindle into silence as if on cue, as plates are collected and the contemplative business of cleaning is begun, sponges and cleanser requested with a gentle gesture.

And what is all this studious self-containment in the service of? Round-the-clock efforts to draw closer to God, and to ask through prayer for help and guidance on behalf of anyone in the world who might be suffering.

While one might assume that the ideal contemplative is someone who is happiest silent and alone, the opposite is true. Spirited extroverts are prized in communities like this, the more "bubbly" and "tomboyish" the better, according to one mother superior in the book *The Nuns*. The inner fortitude implied enables her to cope better with the life. There is proof of this in Greenville's Sister Nancy Shively, who, at fifty-three years old, is gregarious, intellectual, playfully sacrilegious on occasion, armed with a rapid-fire laugh that is liberally deployed during periods of recreation. Her haircut is short and efficient, something a swimmer might wear, and her mouth is always on the verge of grinning. Not exactly a pious church mouse. She also happens to be the sister with a glass eye. It is slightly colder and less mobile than her real eye, giving Sister Nancy the intriguing look of someone who always has something else on her mind—someone who is vastly more than her affable surface suggests.

"I'm living in an environment where my day can be centered around the relationship that means the most to me," she explains. "And isn't that what everybody wants, really? You get married because you want to focus your life on that person. You want to spend time with your spouse, and you have to work at making that happen. I'm very blessed to live in an environment where we all have the same priority and we all make it happen."

Sister Nancy's day begins when she wakes up on her own at about 3:30 A.M., which gives her almost four hours before morning prayer to worship privately, read, and exercise. "Then I feel like my day has the right foundation," she says. "It's kind of like eating your Wheaties." The idea of prayer as a fortifying, physical experience isn't uncommon. Another sister likens her private morning prayer to "spiritual Drano": "It opens up your pipes so that you can be in tune with God throughout the day," she says, and laughs. "Oh, that's terrible!"

Sister Nancy values the fact that the first words she speaks out loud each day are words of praise. She is talking about the Divine Office. And while Sister Nancy participates wholeheartedly, she admits that this rote ritual isn't her favorite way to pray. A fair number of contemplatives are ambivalent about the sometimes bloodless recitations of psalms and prayers that can be dry, irrelevant, and often militaristic: "Blessed be the Lord, my rock who trains my hands for war, my fingers for battle" (Ps. 144:1). As one Poor Clare in formation put it in an unguarded moment, "Some of those psalms suck!" Still, most nuns respect the Divine Office for its universality: Somewhere in the world at pretty much any moment of the day, there are Christians hoisting their hearts and voices toward God.

But Sister Nancy is happiest worshipping in the most unscripted of ways. "I love our retreat days, when I can put on dungarees and a sweatshirt and go outside to the hermitage and just kind of live by my own rhythm," she says. "I'll take my Walkman and go out to the cemetery and dance." When she is out in nature, a gentle breeze feels like the caress of God. "Or sometimes I just lie on the floor in the chapel and pray. I love to do that." As for the actual content of her, or any nun's, solitary prayer, there are endless varieties. "The way I begin prayer most often is, 'God, tell me, who are You, and who am I? Who are You, and who am I? Teach me' "—this in a limpid, transfixing tone of voice. "And then I just listen. Usually I don't hear anything, like hear-hear," she says, well aware that howling silences are just part of the deal.

"Sometimes I use the Jesus prayer," she continues. "It's like a chant: 'Jesus, Son of God have mercy on me, Jesus, Son of God have mercy on me, Jesus, Son of God have mercy on me.' I just repeat that over and over. I either sit in the Blessed Sacrament chapel in the dark, or I sit in my room and light a candle. I also like incense and quiet music with flute and harp"—anything to enable her disengagement from the ploddingly concrete, temporal realm and her subsequent entry into the warm bath of contemplation. Other times she will practice what is called centering prayer, where one chooses a word like "love" or "Jesus" or "yes," focusing on it so intensely that the word itself obliterates the day's mundane particulars like a spark burning an old photograph to its edges. "And sometimes I just say, 'Okay, God, here I am. I'm not in very great shape today, but it's the best I can do. Just do with me what You will.' " While other nuns stare at pictures of Jesus when they pray, Sister Nancy never conjures up a specific image; she says she isn't visual and couldn't picture the color red if she had to. For her, when prayer is working, God is something vast and enveloping—"like the air we breathe," as another nun puts it. Teresa of Ávila once said that prayer is like being in a dark room with a friend: You can't see the friend, but you know the friend is there.

While some prayer takes the form of a declarative plea for help, much of contemplative prayer is just this: a meditative collecting of the spirit and a centering of the soul that renders the sister open and available to God. Any Poor Clare hopes to effect change in the world with ardent prayer, but she also aims simply to live a life of peace and grace as a symbol of God's love. As one unprofessed Poor Clare put it, "I was always a doer. Then I came here and I had to learn to be a be-er."

On Monday morning the nuns have assembled for the welcoming of a woman named Bernadette into the community as a novice. There is a flower box full of daffodils and crocuses at the foot of the lectern and a sister taking pictures with an Instamatic camera. At a certain point Sister Bernadette, a smallish, pleasant-looking woman in her fifties, reads, "God's call is irrevocable. God has led me through many deserts, wildernesses as well as oases. I am convinced that God has led me to this monastery. Therefore I ask today to begin my novitiate in this Poor Clare community. By the grace of God may I live my days here as a Poor Clare in poverty, chastity, obedience, and enclosure. Knowing I cannot do this alone, I ask to be clothed with the habit of a Poor Clare and to be received as sister into your lives."

After adding a few words about the significance of the day,

the abbess, Sister Rucia, hands Sister Bernadette a rectangular basket that contains her habit: a piece of folded cloth and a knotted rope, absent the crown of thorns that is still worn in some Poor Clare communities. Yesterday during Mass a jolly, voluble priest swathed in a majestic purple vestment called a chasuble blessed the habit. Standing in front of the basket and reading the blessing from a piece of paper tucked into a plastic sleeve, he shook an aspergillum, which looks something like a vintage ice-cream scoop, and sprinkled the habit with the holy water contained within the aspergillum's perforated bulb. In a closed and self-sufficient community like this, it seems odd that an outsider would have to be called in for such formalities. This priest doesn't live among the sisters and has no special attachments to them. His sensibility and theirs hardly seem compatible, as when he indulged in a silly joke during Mass. (Having been invited to a parishioner's house for dinner, the priest asks the woman's son what they will be having. "Goat," the boy replies. "Are you sure?" says the priest. "Yeah, I heard Mom say it was time to have the old goat for dinner." Most of the nuns laughed politely.)

But by the next day's "clothing ceremony," which doesn't require a priest, the community's insulating intimacy has been restored. It is just the sisters admitting another into their ranks. When she receives the basket containing the habit, Sister Bernadette walks to the back of the choir and out. While she is gone, the sisters emerge from the choir stalls and line the space between them. Then Sister Bernadette comes back in, transformed—wearing the habit, smiling, with tears in her eyes. There is mild laughter and a big smile on every face. Sister Bernadette goes around the room receiving hugs and whispered blessings,

"I love yous" muffled in a crush of habits. Tissues materialize from pockets and sisters wipe their eyes. More pictures. Someone says to Sister Bernadette, "You're fixing to lose your cord"—its knots are beginning to slip through the loop. She laughs. "I'll get used to it," Sister Bernadette says.

At the end of the ceremony the sisters crowd around Sister Bernadette and lay on hands: Anxious fingers reach in for a forearm, a hip, one of her shoulders; one hand stretches to reach the top of Sister Bernadette's head. Then they chant the blessing of St. Clare, followed by a hymn:

> *O Lord, You are the center of my life.*
> *I will always praise You.*
> *I will always serve You.*
> *I will always keep You in my sight.*

The fact that only a male priest can say Mass and bless their habits rankles some of these Poor Clares. For them it can be a challenge reconciling this ancient, patriarchal way of life with their feminism. The community has such a different spirit from some of the pre–Vatican II monasteries and convents wherein novices were schooled and groomed by pious, bullying elders. Here the women enter in their thirties and forties and are brought along by peers in the gentlest way; public humiliations and punishments are avoided. In this Poor Clare community one finds self-aware adults cohabiting peacefully for the most part, making their own rules in many cases, and ignoring practices that seem stuffy and outdated. Some of the women are in favor of the ordination of women and the use of inclusive language in the liturgy. Sister Nancy even jokes about blessing the holy water herself if a priest isn't handy, not that she ever has; she illustrates by waving her hands like a second-rate magician over an imaginary vessel.

"When I used to work in a parish, sometimes people would come to me after Mass and they would say, 'Sister, I have this Bible or this rosary, would you bless it for me?' " she remembers. "It seemed funny, because I thought most people would want a priest, but sure, why can't I bless it? Of course I'll bless it. I'd say, 'Lord, bless this,' and I'd make the sign of the cross and give it to them—'There, it's blessed'—and they'd be happy." Sacrilegious as that might seem, Sister Nancy is less intent on subverting the church than she is on not being diverted by pointless pomp from what, in her assessment, really matters.

When Sister Nancy took her final vows and became a fully professed member of this Poor Clare community, she put together a photo album of the dramatic day. It resembles nothing so much as a wedding album, with its photographs of primly attired old friends and family who had flown in for the ceremony. The big difference is that where one might find photographs of the marrying couple clasping hands and going through the paces of the ritual together, Sister Nancy is pictured alone—receiving, but not giving, a fourteen-karat-gold ring. Signifying her lifelong commitment, it looks and functions like a wedding ring, although closer inspection reveals a tiny crucifix upon it, radiating rays. Tucked into the album are congratulatory cards, including one from the abbess, Sister Rucia. In closing, her message says, "I look forward to growing old together."

That is a profound dividend. By entering this community, women elect to spend the rest of their days with like-minded women, marking time in a quiet, controlled way that masks the radicalism of a life that's been shorn of all the usual comforts and pleasures. While the absence of men and children appears to be their most drastic sacrifice, it might be the endless, grinding cycle of silence and prayer that is, to the outsider, the most fundamentally alien, given its absence of measurable results.

At a certain point during prayer, members of the community extemporaneously send up intercessory prayers—requests for people in need. "For all the people traveling today, let us pray." Then the community intones, "Lord, hear our prayer." "For all the people who might be incarcerated, taking the blame for something their brother did, we pray." "Lord, hear our prayer." "For people who have no one praying for them today, let us pray." "Lord, hear our prayer." The solo voice is thin as smoke, floating up; the rejoinder is leaden. Does any of this help? How could it possibly?

While anguished laypeople wonder what kind of a God would let young mothers throw newborns in trash cans and psychopaths shoot at children in a playground, most nuns are quick to point out that God doesn't control us and that the existence of evil in the world is a fact of life. So if God isn't in the business of stilling the hand of the murderer before he strikes, why pray? To an outsider the answers are frustratingly murky. Some contemplatives explain that prayer is less about attempting to rig fate than it is about finding a way to accept it. "Prayer changes you more than it changes what's going to happen," says Sister Rucia. "Hopefully, it gives you a greater acceptance of whatever does happen, and that there is some good that's going to come out of this, even if it's not the way you would prefer it to be right now. There is a growing trust that we are in God's hands." To be sure, belief in heaven is the ultimate comfort in the face of relentless earthly tragedy. "I don't look at this life as our only life," one nun says. "It's such a small portion of eternity, of a total, wonderful life with God."

Yet such vagaries are frequently coupled with unalloyed pragmatism. Sister Rucia also says, "You want to help, and you realize there's only so much you can do with your two hands. And prayer—if you have that faith in prayer—opens up so many possibilities. We're not here just for ourselves."

This is a departure from the traditional monastic paradigm in which the nun focuses primarily on the state of her relationship with God. Along with working and praying on mankind's behalf, her chief aim is to save her own soul and earn a place in God's kingdom. Perfecting that relationship and securing that eternal place is her purpose. Communal yet personal, informed by a vertical model of our relationship to God, this was the prevailing mode of prayer before Vatican II. Hence the ban on reading material containing potentially distracting news of the outside world. (When one young postulant in a very strict order was asked by her mother superior what she would miss most about secular life, the postulant quite sincerely replied, "The Sunday *Times.*") Typically only the most dramatic news ever made it over the walls, like the fact that a man had traveled to the moon or that the United States was going to war. But even information of that magnitude was often sketchily transmitted. One former Trappistine remembers being in the barn when another nun raced in red-faced, gesturing madly, forming a pistol with her fingers and shoving her middle finger in the air—the dubious symbol in Cistercian sign language for "the person in charge." After much silent confusion the nun got the message that President Kennedy had been shot.

These days in many convents and monasteries, certain newspapers and magazines and even television news are permitted. The otherwise very traditional Benedictine nuns on Shaw Island are so devoted to Peter Jennings's broadcast, they have taken an interest in the newsman's personal life and well-being ("Poor man," says Mother Hildegard. "He must have a very dissipated life. Which wife is he on?"). Most sisters have come to realize that they need to know what's going on outside the monastery if they are going to pray effectively. Amid the worldwide drama, some nuns see themselves as serving an essential and concrete function. "To me it's like prayer is our job," one of the Poor Clare postulants puts it. "That's what we do here: We pray for the world. And when we come together to pray, it's kind of like we're working together, just like women working in the kitchen. We're all in this together, and we're all looking at each other in the choir as we do our work. When I pick up my breviary"—the book of psalms, hymns, and prayers that the sisters use each day during the Liturgy of the Hours—"I always think, 'This is my tool that I work with.' " Yet even this sister tempers her can-do attitude with the belief that living as Clare and being as contemplative and close to God as possible is the real purpose and beauty of this life. "It's not so important what we do," she says, "but who we are."

Cloistered, communal life is a delicate balance of preferences and personalities. Contemplative nuns frequently point out that they live with many women who wouldn't necessarily be their first choice for a housemate, let alone friend. But they say that is one of their edifying challenges. Learning to be less petty, angry, jealous, exclusive, and, above all, judgmental is basic to becoming a good nun.

The absence of material possessions unites the women by eliminating differences in circumstance. One postulant from a semi-cloistered order that allows two weeks of vacation tells of asking the prioress if she could spend hers in Europe, if her brother pays her way. The prioress said no, explaining that "not everybody has a brother who can do that." "We live in common, and one sister's room can't be luxurious, with miniblinds and all kinds of stuff while another has nothing," says the postulant. "Community life is a witness for the world that different types of people with different personalities can live together as one." At their best, contemplative communities approximate families in all their complexities and enduring rewards. In Rumer Godden's 1969 novel *In This House of Brede*, a veteran nun comforts a lonely newcomer with this: "Go down to the bottom of the garden, and turn and see the lights and think of the warmth of interest and companionship we have here—and everything we need. Then think of those who have nothing, the truly lonely, the sick, the refugees. That will make you feel better."

Yet the goal of peaceful coexistence within a monastery or convent isn't always easily achieved. Something as mundane as whether the window in a common space should be left open or closed is the kind of issue that can fester and ultimately polarize sisters. And if a single member is unwilling to compromise, the fabric of the community can easily snag and fray.

Among the Greenville Poor Clares, community business is handled in an entirely democratic fashion. Pretty much everything is voted on—which means there will always be some who aren't happy with the outcome. For instance, in the early nineties it was decided that the community would read a revised version of the Liturgy of the Hours that uses feminine and gender-neutral pronouns. While some members were uncomfortable with this politically tinged change, all of the sisters abide by it.

A community custom like this one is negotiable. What is not negotiable is the nun's commitment to God and prayer: Anyone who comes up short in these areas will quickly disrupt the gestalt of the group. Albeit marching to her own drummer, an extraordinarily singular Poor Clare named Sister Mary Lucy Reynolds is in no way considered such a disruption, thanks to the strength of her spirituality. Sister Mary Lucy is one of the few remaining founders of this community—one of twelve who left an overflowing family of Poor Clares in the Boston area on a windy night in 1955 and flew to Greenville to set down roots here. There are only three of the original twelve sisters left (two quit the community, and the other seven died; seven plain white crosses mark their graves in the small cemetery out in the yard, where every member of this community will one day be buried). As one of the few who still wears a veil and embodies the history of the place, Sister Mary Lucy is kind of a cherished relic—a real emblem of the constancy of the life. Now nearing seventy and almost blind, she is taking her commitment a step further.

With the blessing of the other sisters, Sister Mary Lucy is heeding a call to the hermitic life: spending the better part of her day in a camper on the property referred to as the hermitage, and communing with God in intensive and solitary silence. Knowing every twist and turn in this place as well as she does, Sister Mary Lucy finds her way back inside for communal prayer now and then so that she can be in the presence of the Blessed Sacrament. At such times her head drops low and tilts sharply, her eyes tiny and closed like horizontal crescents as she listens to the psalms she knows so well. She is that rare sort of religious who really seems to be radiating something—holiness or contentment, perhaps. Despite the fact that she regularly retreats from the rhythm of the group, Sister Mary Lucy's call is valued and upheld by the others, as she contributes a prayerful energy that is said to be palpable. "You feel it," one of the sisters says. "You really do."

While accommodations will always be made for a spiritual force like Sister Mary Lucy, some women who do not fit the mold will never make it in a community like this. Divorced women and widows tend not to make good candidates. Some have children, and their inalterable identity as a mother makes for divided loyalties. As Sister Rucia says, "We've not had a lot of success with that." Understandably, since the nun who is also a mother is essentially juggling two callings. One divorced, middle-aged mother of two in a semicloistered nursing order attested to the difficulty of being allowed to see her grown children no more than once a year. In lighter moments, her son called her "Sister Mom." The woman applied herself heroically to the challenges of the novitiate. But having concluded that she is more mother than nun, she quit the order after less than two years.

Women with apparent psychological problems are rarely permitted to enter a community like the Poor Clares. Anyone prone to depression, for instance, can throw the community off balance. But many disorders cannot be anticipated or avoided, as in the case of the Poor Clare who developed Alzheimer's before she died. In the early stages her illness manifested as mischief. If anything in the monastery was missing, it could be found in her pockets or in her room. Other nuns had to look after her at all times—shooing imaginary people off her bed and giving her large piles of buttons to sort out; the next day the buttons would be mixed up and given back to her. Frequently the sister lost her false teeth, prompting terrible concern that they'd been packed in with altar breads that were en route to some parish. Sometimes in chapel she'd begin ripping pages from her prayer book; occasionally she came out of her room wearing nothing. Caring for such a sick sister was an act of love, but it was also very stressful in a community powered by methodical labors, contemplation, and silence. At least now the sisters can search out medical help. A few decades ago the concept of enclosure was so strict, they were entirely reliant on house calls. The monastery even had its own dentist chair. Ultimately, however, dentists and doctors refused to work under such questionable conditions.

This life isn't easily preserved. Perhaps most taxing is the realization that concessions will have to be made to modernity. Already the Greenville Poor Clares have an exercise room filled with fancy donated equipment like a NordicTrack, a stationary bike, and a StairMaster. Decades ago a feature of monastic life was the total denial of one's physical state. Part of the point of the voluminous habit was to hide the nun's body from herself and everyone else, while illness and food preferences were all but ignored. The premium on uniformity so outweighed personal tastes that even in this Poor Clare community, women of all shapes and sizes were required to eat the exact same amount of food at every meal. Now, however, the sisters acknowledge the importance of good health, vigorous exercise, and even a tiny bit of vanity (one nun's eyebrows are artfully plucked).

The sisters are also computer-savvy now, and some programs can be exceedingly helpful. They'll go on-line for recipes and consumer information—for instance, if the monastery is shop-ping for an efficient and inexpensive appliance. Their knowledge of desktop publishing has allowed them to be creative with prayer cards and mailings, both of which are important ways of raising funds. The sisters used to sustain themselves making altar breads, which involved pouring a water-and-flour mixture into a waffle iron the size of a mangle and cutting the sheets into hundreds of tiny circles. But there are big companies now that mass-produce the breads, and the sisters just can't compete with them. Computers have opened up other opportunities. (One cloistered community used to have a room called the Scripto-rium, where sisters earned money for the monastery by doing calligraphy jobs. Eventually the trade died out when pens and paper were replaced by a Macintosh computer, so naturally the room was renamed the Mactorium.)

Yet computers don't seem conducive to contemplation. What about the vast and chatty world that one is connected to via the Internet? How does one maintain the spirit of enclosure when the virtual world is a click away? Of course, the sisters aren't likely to indulge in the Internet's tawdrier offerings. It is up to them to stay focused on God and limit their excursions into cyberspace, just as one had to rein in a wandering mind in the days before (and since) computers. Still, the silence of computer work can be deceiving.

Sister Rucia admits that the Poor Clares have to reach out to the Greenville community if they are going to survive. Their early benefactors are dying off, and they need to spark support for their mission. While they aren't about to approach people with begging bowls, the sisters' mendicant origins are very much alive in their ongoing dependence on the generosity of outsiders.

Yet how to solicit help without betraying their purpose? The sisters can't very well host open houses and join civic groups; they can't become local personalities, like the proprietors of used-car dealerships. But they have to do something. Ironically, they have to reach out in order to remain separate. They have to keep changing in order to preserve their essence. They have to find a way to protect the space where they pray.

For contemplative nuns like the Poor Clares, prayer is the utter sustenance of their lives. For many active sisters, it is a quick snack, gobbled on the run. "I pray in the shower or in the car," says Donna Quinn, the Dominican sister who works in a homeless shelter in Chicago and whose rhetoric runs more toward the political than the spiritual. "That's my prayer life. Those are quiet moments when I can think about my God. I also find incredible spirituality and prayer with the little kids at the shelter hugging me, grabbing my knees, and the women coming up and slapping me on the back or saying 'I need help.' That is my spiritual life." As a post–Vatican II formulation, this notion of prayer isn't all that radical. In the council's determination to bring the church to the people, the idea that you could see the face of Jesus Christ in the face of your neighbor, not just in your mind's eye or in an icon's plaster gaze, gained strength. It legitimized so many nuns' desire to break out of the convent and work among the people.

Members of apostolic orders often say they are grateful for the cloistered nuns who do so much of the spiritual work, throwing more coal on the fire in the engine room, in essence fueling the active sisters' practical labors out in the world. Which isn't to say active communities ever entirely abandoned the idea of formal prayer, even if it has become a difficult obligation to fulfill. "We are asked to spend an hour in prayer every morning, which I do," says Margaret Traxler, the outspoken School Sister of Notre Dame whose ministry has been in prisons and shelters. "And I find that I have to do it early, otherwise I don't get to it during the day. Sometimes I think it's a luxury. But I mustn't say that, because I know it is something I need. And somehow it brings the whole former day into proper focus and helps me focus on the day ahead. It's important."

The unschooled need only give prayer a try to realize how difficult it really is. If the nun prepares her mind for prayer by emptying it—turning it into a stark white room—the secular mind is as busy as a pinball machine. In our self-consciousness the words grow hollow, their meaning obscured by the funny sound of them. Our doubts about God can lead to an incapacitating tentativeness. There is that pull to distraction, that curious looking back and around that would prove fatal to the tightrope walker but in the amateur pray-er merely breaks the mood and allows all manner of earthly skepticism to flood in.

Bowed head, clasped hands, trembling lips, and sore knees—this is what most of us picture when we think of prayer. However, the quest for God is so personal a mission, some sisters have found their own ways of reaching out.

Martha Ann Kirk, a Sister of Charity of the Incarnate Word who teaches at the University of the Incarnate Word in San Antonio, Texas, has drawn fans and raised eyebrows with her avid promotion of mime, movement, and liturgical dance—that is, dance as prayer. Some traditionalists decry the flamboyance and sensuality of liturgical dance. As they see it, prayer should be dignified and private. But for Sister Martha Ann, connecting with God can and perhaps should be an exhilarating, sponta-neous, full-body experience. Bringing a decidedly feminist fla-vor to the proceedings, she leads workshops and classes in which Bible stories are acted out in sweeping, emotional, mod-ern dancelike movements designed to stir and loose deep devo-tional feelings.

One such workshop took place at the Women's Ordination Conference in Washington, D.C., in 1995. Speakers included the prominent feminist theologian Elisabeth Schussler-Fiorenza, as well as Sister of Mercy Theresa Kane, who has been all but can-onized by feminist sisters for bringing their cause to Pope John Paul II during his visit to the United States in 1979. Then presi-dent of the Leadership Council of Women Religious, she was invited to greet him when he addressed five thousand women religious in Washington, D.C. Everyone there was stunned when Sister Theresa actually said to the pope, "I urge you, Your Holi-ness, to be open to and respond to the voices coming from the women of this country who are desirous of serving in and through the Church as fully participating members." (When she finished, the pope blessed her and the program continued.)

In the intensely feminist spirit of the ordination conference, Sister Martha Ann's liturgical-dance workshop was called "Dancing a Discipleship of Equals." Standing in the center of a sterile function room in a large hotel, Sister Martha Ann—then in her late forties—asked the participants to come join her in a cir-cle. Rising up softly on the balls of her bare feet, holding her lim-ber torso straight and high, she drew everyone in with outstretched arms and an impossibly sweet smile. Wearing a purple sweater and a gauzy, shin-length skirt, her long, blond-gray hair grazing her hips as she moved, Sister Martha Ann lowered the lights while a guitarist began to slap the wood of her instrument rhythmically, pounding out a heartbeat. Then Sister Martha Ann closed her eyes and "bless[ed] the space," proclaiming it a womb in which all could feel safe. She went around the room, asking each person's name, then chanting it, between the dirgelike refrain "You are beloved by God."

The guitarist proceeded to sing a sad song about the beleaguered women of the world—the Indian girl who has to walk miles to fill her vessel with water, the African woman who was forced as a child to have a clitoridectomy. The participants were instructed to feel these women's pain and even to act it out, if they could, although some could only swing and twirl around the multicultural altar of mirrored fabrics, shawls, finger cymbals, bells, and candles. As they cast about, Sister Martha Ann chanted in falsetto, "There are people in the world who can't get water, yet we can get a bomb anywhere in the world in under two minutes. Could we find a way to get water to people who need it?" Then she dipped her fingers into a glass of water and streaked each person's cheeks with "tears."

This is prayer? Well, yes, Sister Martha Ann would emphatically say. Armed with a doctorate in theology and the arts, she energetically refutes the notion that mime and dance are faddish and fringe, and therefore somehow lesser ways to worship. Physicality in prayer has a long and rich tradition. She cites the ecstatic dance of the Sufis, as well as Buddhism, in which breathing and an acute awareness of one's physical state are essential.

Furthermore, she points out, early Christians danced in circles, emulating the angels that were said to dance around the throne of God. "Constantly in the Bible they talk about raising hands in prayer," Sister Martha Ann says. "And the traditional liturgy has a lot of bowing and kneeling and beating your breast." A liturgical-dance guide she wrote opens with a reference to the passage from the Book of Exodus in which the prophetess Miriam "took a tambourine in her hand; and all the women went out after her with tambourines and with dancing," while singing songs in praise of God.

For her own part, Sister Martha Ann describes liturgical dancing as being "totally caught up in the experience of prayer. It's like doing exercise. When you're tired and you're stressed and then you do this, you sweat and you're exhilarated and you feel freed. I think dance in worship can function like that," she says, alluding to the link between body and soul. After all, the concept of Incarnation, in which the Divine became flesh in the form of Jesus Christ, is a kind of theological justification for a body-soul symbiosis. "In teaching meditation I tell my students, 'If you are very resistant to prayer and God, at least just try to pray with your palms open and see if that will help you open your mind and your heart more.' Our bodies can lead us."

Encouraging distracted college students to apply their physical energies to Christ and inhabit His experience isn't always easy, but it is Sister Martha Ann's job to try.

A balmy spring Wednesday finds her in the University of the Incarnate Word's majestic chapel, patrolling the space like a director. With only two days left until their performance on Good Friday, her "Arts for Christian Worship" class is working out the kinks in their passion mime, the story of Christ's death and resurrection acted out.

Clenching a pencil between her teeth, Sister Martha Ann walks toward the altar where the mime is taking place, her long black flowing skirt lifting gently on the breeze as she goes. She has that typical dancer's posture, honed by years of training and classes: spine straight, face tilted up, feet splayed slightly, steps measured and light. "Mary," she says to a student whose head is draped in blue cloth, "you need to be able to see Jesus out of the corner of your eye and grasp Him when his head drops. Jesus, do like you're dying." As a boy in a backward baseball cap wilts, some girls in jeans help him to the floor and cover him with a cloth. A few moments later the boy rises, tosses the cloth over his shoulder like a gym bag, and walks off. Sister Martha Ann suggests that he execute his resurrection a tad more reverently.

Afterward she gathers the class and asks how this particular run-through felt. "Monday I thought you were still thinking it," she says. "But today I felt that you were starting to pray it, and that's great." Before they disperse, Sister Martha Ann gathers the students for a more traditional kind of prayer—the kind one sees sports teams gathering for on the heels of a big victory. As they reach out for one another's hands, one girl apologizes that hers might still be dirty from soccer practice.

How someone as ethereal and self-styled as Sister Martha Ann came of age in the regimented institutional church is difficult to imagine. The way she flips and flings around her waist-length hair seems almost like a pointed repudiation of the old ways that found nuns hacking off their locks or shaving their heads, compulsively tucking errant strands under their wimple. Nonetheless, she has joined a system predicated on strict forms and rules, like that found in the breviary:

If the Office of Readings is said immediately before another Hour of the Office, then the appropriate hymn for that Hour may be sung at the beginning of the Office of Readings. At the end of the Office of Readings the prayer and conclusion are omitted, and in the Hour following the introductory verse with the *Glory to the Father* is omitted.

Presumably such painstaking regulations are intended to pre-empt the improvisations of a Sister Martha Ann.

She bears no trace of the archetypal spare and tidy novice whose training was very much about staying within boundaries. Sister Martha Ann's office at the university is heaped with books, files, and yellowed, stapled pages; wads of paper are bursting from desk drawers that barely close. Her Geo hatchback is a rolling prop-closet. Describing her love of dance, Sister Martha Ann once said, "I have always felt very free in my body and enjoyed my body"—a sentiment that might have some pre–Vatican II sisters rolling in their graves. Within the bounds of this institution, Sister Martha Ann has always been her own person—which is to say, a person who has struggled.

One summer at the convent, she was making batiks, designs on fabric created with wax and dye. "I was in a little room in the basement where we did our mending," she remembers, "and I was just having such a wonderful time, all caught up in these wonderful colors and designs. So the director of students called me in. I expected to get comments on all the beautiful artwork that was hanging around. Instead I was reprimanded for dripping wax on the floor and messing up the convent. Another time I had a wonderful concept for Easter, to make huge butterflies, which are a symbol of resurrection, out of bright colored paper and hang them on invisible fishing line over the altar." Describing something like this, which, to Sister Martha Ann, is kind of brilliant and delicious, she squints and rubs her fingertips together rapidly on either hand, feeling for the essence of the thing, searching for the perfect word. "So we hung about twenty or thirty bright, beautiful, huge butterflies. At the same time some of the older sisters were having their twenty-fifth and fiftieth anniversary of their vows, and they were to have a special solemn Mass in the chapel. So they said they wanted all of those junky butterflies taken down for the Mass." She deflates; her face falls—suddenly she looks about ten years older. "It just devastated me that they couldn't see the beauty of them."

In the novitiate Sister Martha Ann was a free spirit in what amounted to spiritual boot-camp, where every moment of the day was accounted for and minutiae mattered greatly. "We were taught to tuck the sheet into your bed this way, and put your clothes in the bureau this way, and pin on your headdress this way," she remembers. "The assistant to the novice directress would say, 'Keep the rule and the rule keeps you.' And, 'The more faithful you are to all these little things, the closer you are to God.' Some people had scrupulosity breakdowns: 'I can't put everything perfectly in place, so I must be a sinner, and I'm going crazy trying to concentrate on all this stuff!' But I let the pettiness go through the strainer, and I kept the sense of loving and striving for bigger, more essential things."

She had faith in her faith, even as a child. "But was it really an intellectual identification with Catholicism," she says, "or was the experience alluring to my artistic sensibilities? The color of the stained glass, the smell of the incense, the profound sound of the chanting, the poetry of the liturgical text." Later, when she was fourteen, she attended a cousin's graduation at the University of the Incarnate Word, which included a baccalaureate Mass in a Romanesque chapel lined with stained-glass windows beneath a barrel-vaulted ceiling. "I remember thinking, 'This is so beautiful, I could pray here forever.' But again, was I just responding to the lights and colors and smells and music and sense of awe?"

If Sister Martha Ann was drawn in by the trappings, it was the spirituality that made her stay. She is that rare person who seems to dwell in a prayerful state. That is where she is most at home. Even in Catholic school, at the age of eight or nine, while the other children were enjoying recess, Sister Martha Ann (then Martha Sue) would head off to church to sneak in a few minutes of prayer. "Then I would go out and play with everyone else," she says. "But it was very precious to me to have these little chats with God where I'd say, 'This is how I am' or 'Take care of my grandmother who just had a stroke.' I loved the quiet of the church." In the fifth grade she started saying the prayer of St. Francis on her own every day: "Lord, make me an instrument of Your peace. Where there is hatred, let me sow love; where there is injury, pardon; where there is doubt, faith; where there is despair, hope; where there is darkness, light; where there is sadness, joy. . . ." By the time Martha Sue was in the eighth grade, she was going to Mass every day, unless her family was on vacation or far from a church. "It was really important and really beautiful to me. Momma and Daddy didn't quite understand my need to get up and do this, but they didn't stop me. I had a sort of deep devotion to the Eucharist—a sense of intimacy with Christ.

"There has never been a time that prayer was real, real hard for me, or a real, real struggle," she says. "And maybe that has something to do with being more of an introvert. It's sort of nice to be able to slip away and be quiet." She still does so today. At the house she shares with three other Incarnate Word sisters in a Hispanic neighborhood on the edge of downtown San Antonio, it isn't surprising to find Sister Martha Ann up late at night, sitting in the lotus position in the dark on the floor of their tiny makeshift chapel, engaged in deep and wordless conversation.

Yet her prayerful constancy, her peaceful drift into the lulling eternal, is frequently interrupted by the timeliest concerns: Sister Martha Ann has a flinty disdain for church politics, and she hasn't been shy about challenging the old order. As a young nun around the time of Vatican II, her willingness to experiment with a slightly shorter habit earned her the racy nickname "Martha Miniskirt" among her students. Now her image of God frequently assumes a feminine cast: There are times during prayer that she has the sense of "being in the womb of God" or being rocked in God's arms like a baby by its mother. "There is that recurring sense for me in my prayer, that sense of a nurturing God, a protective God" in whose loving care she is renewed and reborn.

It is a radical idea, in the eyes of the church. But then other equally radical challenges to the status quo have, over time, become the norm. "I entered in '62," says Sister Martha Ann. "Soon after, the priest gave a strong sermon saying, 'The Roman Catholic Church has to have Latin. Latin unifies us and is central in our tradition.' That was in September. In December, Vatican II announces we can use different languages and vernacular in worship. So right off I was skeptical of these pronouncements about universal traditions." In other words, if Latin—and the traditional habit—can be deemed inessential, then what about the rule that says only men can be priests?

There are many such questions, and no satisfying answers. Sister Martha Ann got an early taste of the church's systemic sexism during graduate school, when she found out that a priest she knew was working toward a licentiate, official Vatican permission to teach theology, according to Sister Martha Ann. "I thought, 'Gosh, he and I are both enrolled in doctoral studies, but he's also getting a licentiate; I'm going to apply for one of those, too.' " But when she inquired, the administrator who happened to be a priest told her they hadn't given licentiates in years, and he didn't know if they'd ever give them again. "So I went back to my friend and said, 'Did I misunderstand that you're getting a licentiate at the same time that you're getting a doctorate?' And then he showed me a letter that said, 'When you have completed so many hours of theology and taken x comprehensive exams, you will be awarded the licentiate.' The letter was from the priest that I had spoken to face-to-face. I was absolutely furious. I had been lied to by a priest." Apparently the Vatican had called for an inspection of all American seminaries, and the administration was nervous about having it in their records that a number of women were receiving licentiates, on top of theology degrees. "I felt so angry and so betrayed. I fought it for over a year, going from one administrator to another, and I really was bruised and bloodied." Sister Martha Ann never did receive the licentiate.

That debacle presaged the losing battle that is still at the heart of Sister Martha Ann's religious life. She feels called to the priesthood. She has lived as an instrument of prayer and knows that her role is to lead people in worship and perform sacred rites. But almost certainly she will never be allowed to answer that call. For her this is a tragedy—as devastating as infertility would be to the woman who longs to bear a child.

By way of therapy as much as instruction, she devised a

cathartic drama that springs from the fact that women were the first to encounter the risen Christ. The Lord charges them with the task of spreading the news to His disciples. In the mime dance Sister Martha Ann, as one of those female messengers whom the disciples don't take seriously, looks at her own hands and sees wounds like those on Christ. "And I start to realize that in my woundedness, in my pain, in the struggles I have gone through, I really know what resurrection is about." Sister Martha Ann starts to weep. "And *I* can proclaim reconciliation, and *I* can proclaim healing, and *I* can proclaim getting up and going on." Just like a priest.

Despite her frustration, Sister Martha Ann makes do, and every now and then makes light. When she received her doctorate, some friends wanted to give her a graduation party. When she arrived, she saw that the backyard was decorated and people were in costumes, singing, laughing, and praying. Something was afoot. "What they were doing was preparing to make me a bishop," Sister Martha Ann says. "A Jesuit priest friend and some seminarians and these crazy Loretto nuns I knew had gotten hold of the official Roman Catholic ritual for ordaining a bishop and had rewritten the prayer. For instance, a bishop is given a ring as his insignia of office. Well, they said, 'A ring of friends will gather around you, and this is the insignia of your office.' " And instead of a miter, they placed a wreath of flowers on her head. "There was an anointing and a laying on of hands. It was hysterical and profound and wonderful."

Sister Martha Ann will continue to behave as priestlike as canon law allows. One service at the university chapel finds her giving a homily and distributing Communion while wearing an alb that was stitched by her mother, overlaid with a red appliquéd vestment made by someone in Northern California who sells such items to ordained Protestant women. Holding forth from the ambo, or lectern, this diminutive, self-described introvert is suddenly stretching her arms up and out as if to embrace her flock, her wisdom and compassion rolling out in plummy tones. More than priestly, she looks ineffably serene.

On the morning of Good Friday, Sister Martha Ann is energized by the spirit of the day and its full schedule of holy festivities. The highlight is the passion play that takes place downtown, kind of a grandiose rendition of her students' passion mime. Thousands of Texans have gathered at the Mercado under an oppressive sun to experience the story of Christ's death and resurrection in a life-size, real-time, almost participatory way. Pontius Pilate, in blue and red crushed-velvet robes, is questioning Jesus, typically bearded and longhaired, until shouts of "¡Crucifícalo!" ("Crucify him!") ring out. To a bodeful drumbeat, Jesus is stripped to the waist and sent on his torturous way, wearing a crown of thorns and hauling an eleven-foot cross onto Dolorosa Street, the street of sorrows. The swelling, excited, somewhat agitated crowd falls in behind him, as he is flogged and taunted by spear-carrying guards. It seems Calvary has some of the awesome terror of a bullfight: The crowd is transfixed by the smell of certain death in the air. Jesus' face is sweating and anguished, he stumbles and weaves—either this is a very good actor or the playing of this part is every bit as excruciating as it looks.

A non-Catholic from the frigid Northeast can only view this melodramatic, hugely public embrace of the most violent and tragic of stories with a mounting sense of horror. On some level such a spectacle is as curious as the traditional business of wearing crosses on chains, almost like decorative jewelry. But the rituals and symbols draw regular attention to the story of Christ, ensuring that the faithful will never forget. This life-size retelling allows one to literally step into the story itself and be buffeted by the drama. There is a kind of rolling power to the communal nature of the experience and the clear sense, among the faithful, of ownership of this legacy. Throughout, Sister Martha Ann maintains her approving Mona Lisa smile as she moves with the crowd from station to station. This is her idea of worship: public, physical, and so uninhibited—a traditional and prized mode of expression in Hispanic cultures, which is partly why Sister Martha Ann likes living here. Her ongoing desire to discover "how the Word of God takes flesh in our lives" is supported in San Antonio.

Eventually the crowd stops in front of the eighteenth-century Cathedral of San Fernando. Ropes are looped around either side of the cross and then yanked by several extras. In one swift and shocking movement the cross rises up, with Jesus hanging upon it. On cue he is poked in the ribs with a spear, the tip of which is miked, allowing all to hear him say, "*Dios mío, Dios mío, ¿por qué me has abandonado?*" ("My God, my God, why have You abandoned me?") The crowd stares and grows quiet, waiting for him to die.

Sister Martha Ann checks her wristwatch. "There's going to be a prayer service inside the cathedral, so Jesus ought to die by twelve-thirty."

By the Monday after Easter, normal life has returned. At around 7:00 A.M., Sister Martha Ann and two of her housemates meet for their regular communal prayer in their chapel in a corner room on the second floor. There are woven palms from Mexico, decorative fabric, and a thick red candle on the floor, its flame guttering in the morning stillness. Wind chimes and a train whistle are the only sounds outside. One sister wears shorts, another wears a floral housedress, while Sister Martha Ann is in the sweatpants she slept in. Holding a mug of coffee in both hands, her face puffy with sleep, she sinks to the floor and folds her compact legs beneath her, looking like a college student taking a break from cramming for finals. There is no stained glass here, no pageantry to speak of, but still, the spirit of holiness prevails—so much so that to break the silence would seem just as coarse as telling jokes in an actual church.

The women sit quietly for several minutes, just contemplating privately. Then they turn to their breviaries and do their readings aloud. The day after Easter is momentous in the Catholic faith, with its hopeful promise of new life, new beginnings. But as the sisters begin their intercessions, the grim litany of tragedies is as long as ever. One sister offers prayers for a seriously disfigured young woman she is counseling; another, responding to the day's horrific headlines, asks prayers for the Kosovo refugees who are camping in a muddy field, having been turned away from Macedonia—Easter and the newness of the season notwithstanding. One of the sisters lets out an exhausted laugh. "There's trouble already," she says. The other two laugh as well. Reality is inescapable; it's "back to work!" following yet another rousing Easter, like the day after Labor Day for the nine-to-five crowd. There is still, there is always, so much work to be done.

"God, hear our prayer," the sisters say, as one.

No matter what form someone's prayer takes, the question remains: Who is it for? Is prayer for the man on the street, the orphan in Kosovo, or is it a way for the person praying to accrue God's goodwill and feel closer to the Divine? The answer really depends on the person doing the praying. Asked if prayer influences people and events, Sister Martha Ann says, "In my experience, if I am having real problems with a student, if they are lazy or disruptive, if they are really hard to deal with and if I really care, I just need to go to the chapel for an hour and saturate them with healing, with light, with peace. People would make fun of me for saying this, but I have never done that with a student that there hasn't been a change in our relationship."

One could argue that this is less a question of Divine intervention than a change of consciousness on Sister Martha Ann's part—a hard-won willingness to open her heart to that student. Of course, someone like Sister Rucia of the Poor Clares would say that this, too, is the work of prayer, which ultimately changes the person praying more than it influences events. Sister Martha Ann doesn't object to an entirely secular interpretation. "I say to my students, 'Some of you may not be interested in spirituality, so you might say this is some sort of psychological energy and it doesn't have anything to do with the Divine. I personally believe it does, but yet I am happy to work with persons of goodwill who are coming at this from a psychological perspective."

Improving a student's attitude is a worthwhile endeavor. But what of the epic hardships and tragedies that are the bread and butter of so many contemplatives? Sister Martha Ann also trains her energies on vast populations of the hungry and oppressed, and she checks in regularly with a news group on the Internet devoted to Christian prayer that shares information about people in need around the world and offers spiritual forms of help. Sister Martha Ann doesn't doubt the effectiveness of this kind of prayer. By way of example, she cites the work of a Franciscan community of brothers who have been holding prayer vigils at the Nevada nuclear-test site in the Western Shoshone Territory for almost twenty years. She is convinced that the work of the brothers has slowed the testing, although politicians and other concerned, secular citizens might differ.

But for so many religious, prayer is not a public service. Rather, it is the ultimate self-sustaining act. On Shaw Island, which is at such an extreme physical remove from the problems of the world, the Benedictines return to their new chapel seven times a day like rather elegant migratory birds. (On the farm, they plod; in chapel, they glide.) Some Dominican sisters show up for Mass from time to time, as well as a smattering of islanders. Often it is just the Benedictines. I ask Mother Hildegard if this is a problem. If no one comes, then who is this beautiful and expensive chapel for? She is mildly put out by the question. "It's for the Lord," she says. Mother Hildegard doesn't mean to suggest that she and the other nuns aren't working, most of the time, to alleviate worldwide suffering in their prayers. But she is very clear on the idea that "if you can't save yourself, you can't very well save anyone else."

One night I took a walk with a priest in a rural monastic community. He was asking many wide-eyed questions about New York City. A lot of hungry and homeless people, isn't that right? Why do they stay there? Why not move somewhere warmer and simpler? He sort of shuddered and shook his head at the thought of struggling in such a chaotic, unforgiving environment. I found his naïveté to be nothing short of bewildering. He's in the charity business; isn't he supposed to know about the realities of poor people's lives? Not necessarily, as it turns out. For some people prayer is private. It is between them and God (or at least their community and God). The world is welcome to grind and spin around the quiet stillness of that bond. When asked the purpose of diligent prayer, the priest didn't mention a word about the alleviation of worldwide suffering. It is more the singular business of being with Christ in this life and thus earning a place in His eternal kingdom.

But even in the cloistered life, prayer has its semipublic, communal dimension, during the chanting of the Divine Office. In such an environment the solitary and shared aspects of prayer cannot help but intersect. Like chores and matters of hygiene, prayer—when and how it is done—was, for centuries, carefully regulated. But with Vatican II not even one's deepest, most private dialogue with God went untouched.

Marion, now seventy years old, was a fairly typical candidate for religious life when she entered a Trappistine community in 1953. She grew up in a large, churchgoing Catholic family of modest means, with a strict-disciplinarian father at the helm. When she was about seven, it was little more than the dramatic sight of the nuns in their long robes at the local church that inspired Marion to promise Jesus that one day she would become a nun.

Although the thought remained lodged in her mind, it didn't keep her from getting involved with a boyfriend who turned out to be possessive and abusive. By the time Marion was twenty-three, the convent was looking very attractive—a way out of a bad relationship, at the very least.

She joined the Trappistines, an order distinguished by its austere commitment to a prayerful, cloistered life. It was a profound change of pace for someone as emotional and spontaneous as

Marion. Just for a joke, she arrived at the monastery for the first time with five cigarettes jammed in her mouth. Once there, she pushed the rule of silence to the limit and couldn't resist dancing in the halls of the monastery if the spirit happened to move her. But she was quickly overtaken by the gentle rhythm of the life. She loved it, almost from the start. "I was proud as a peacock when I got my habit," Marion says.

As a lay sister, Marion performed manual labors in the barn and in the fields when she wasn't sewing habits—brown ones for the lay sisters and white ones for the choir sisters, wool for winter and cotton for summer. She also did most of the cooking at the monastery. "We made soup from leftovers because we couldn't throw away anything," she says. "If there were potatoes that were baked, mashed, or fried, I'd put in a lot of celery and onions and make a mashy hashy. It was an Irish community, so we always had a lot of potatoes."

By contrast, the choir sisters concerned themselves almost entirely with the refined and time-consuming business of chanting the Divine Office, which required musical ability as well as a command of Latin. The lay sisters' life, which found them rising for chores at 2:30 A.M., necessitated a completely different style of prayer. So while the choir sisters were in the chapel trilling Gregorian chants, the lay sisters would work through simple rote prayers like the Our Father and endless rounds of Hail Marys. Sometimes they said these deeply ingrained prayers on their own. But they also met throughout the day in the chapter room for a communal worship, which was the backbone of their prayer life.

By the late sixties, changes were sweeping through the monastery. Some were welcome: Now the nuns were allowed to rise at the perfectly slothful hour of 3:30 A.M. They also began wearing white habits like the choir sisters. And it was mercifully decided that they could have some coffee before heading out to the barn.

Still other changes cut to the core of the life. In rethinking the ways of their order, the Cistercians, some of whom are Trappistines, decided that there should be a more unified voice in the monastery. To that end, lay sisters were given an English translation of the choir sisters' psalmody—hardly a unifying innovation, in that the lay sisters were still for the most part reading psalms separately from the choir sisters. In addition, they were instructed to stop saying their rote prayers—the Our Fathers and the Hail Marys. "But that was my life," Marion says helplessly. "The prayer part of it is the whole life.

"I was somebody who loved the Our Father. When I was saying it, Jesus was right there saying it with me, and I loved that so much. It got into every nook and cranny of my soul." Then, suddenly, it was gone. Theoretically, a sister could continue to say the prayers on her own time. But no longer were they recognized in an official way as part of the Office. No longer would they function as the spiritual glue that bonded the lay sisters. "It's no fun saying your prayers by yourself," Marion says. "It's so much more powerful when there's a group. But Reverend Mother said we couldn't. And I was very disappointed. I was brokenhearted."

What followed for Marion was a gradual and ultimately harrowing breakdown. She was tired and teary, and one day she collapsed. Her superiors at the monastery gave her some pills to take. Although she didn't know what they were, she followed orders. "I just slept and dreamed, and I had these terribly vicious sexual dreams," she says. "I was so mixed up. I felt like rotten wood on these pills."

She wanted to leave the community, but Reverend Mother told her no, she had solemn vows—a lifelong commitment, in other words. "She would not listen to me," says Marion. "I'd say, 'I don't like it the way it is.' I was mad they were taking away the prayers that were so beautiful to me. I could not accept it. I was also on this medicine."

Eventually Marion volunteered to help start a new Trappistine community in the West, hoping that with a different superior she would get the help she needed. But it didn't work out that way. She was still anxious, angry, and verbally abusive. Reverend Mother thought that more tasks might keep her in line. So she was given some goats to milk, along with the cooking, sewing, and gardening she was already doing. And she was still taking pills. Marion began to buckle. Finally she was taken to the hospital, where she found out that the pills she was taking were phenobarbitol, a strong sedative no doubt intended to curb her outbursts and other un-nunlike behavior.

Ultimately, at the insistence of her superior, Marion ended up leaving the order that had been her spiritual home for more than thirty years. She was traumatized and scared, with no money, no Social Security, and no adult experience in the lay world. When her family picked her up at the airport, they were shocked by her appearance: Marion was wearing hastily purchased clothes from Goodwill, and her hair was strangely sparse (in the monastery her head had been shaved usually every spring and fall).

With the help of family, Marion began to rebuild her life. Eventually she met a man at a square dance whom she married. She is better now, notwithstanding debilitating trouble with her knees from years of gardening and kneeling in prayer. But the experience with the Trappistines was crushing. Seventeen years later Marion still cries at the thought of it. "It's awful," she says. "Because I gave everything to that community." If she outlives her husband, she thinks she might even try to go back.

Marion's story says a lot about the trials of Vatican II, as well as the severe era just before. That nuns would dutifully take pills without knowing what they were, just because the superior had told them to, suggests an emphasis on obedience that eclipsed good sense. Of course, that obedience extended to one's own private time with God. How and when that time would be used was not for the sister to decide.

In Marion's case she was dependent on the rote prayers. It was her security, her comfort, her path to daily grace. And when it fell away, as so many conventions and rituals of religious life would, she was unmoored. In this she was not alone. As sisters by the thousands left the convent for apostolic adventures in big cities and small villages around the world, communal prayer became less and less feasible. That powerful image from the forties and fifties of phalanxes of professed sisters and novices filing into their chapels was quickly becoming a thing of the past.

And yet the nuns adapted, finding new ways to pray—in twos and threes in boxy apartments at homemade altars beneath crosses fashioned of driftwood and twine, by candlelight in huts, even alone, when they are in the shower reaching for the soap. Because without some kind of prayer, they could not be nuns.

ENTIRELY HIS

Nuns and Sexuality

*I*N THE THIRD CENTURY A BEAUTI-
ful, wellborn Sicilian girl named Agatha chose to devote herself
utterly to Christ. Agatha's choice frustrated many a potential
suitor, although none more so than the governor who tried to
force her into marriage. When she resisted, the governor pursued
the only reasonable course of action: He had her arrested, sent to
a brothel, imprisoned, humiliated, and extravagantly tortured—
specifically, Agatha's breasts were hacked off. Ultimately she
died from the abuse. But for managing to remain faithful to
Christ to the last, she was canonized.

Back when marriage and motherhood were the norm, and alle-

giance to the Roman emperor was the law, independent Christian women lived dangerously, to say the least. Some who suffered especially lurid fates would come to be known as the virgin
martyrs of Christian lore, whose stories lived on as testaments to
the heroism of real faith. That many of the stories (like, possibly,
Agatha's) were apocryphal didn't matter; the triumph of the
spirit over comely female flesh has long been a subject ripe for
myth-making. While contemporary religious may find it difficult
to identify with these semihysterical tales, the trials of the virgin
martyrs presaged the countercultural cast of the modern nun.

American women today aren't likely to be tortured for choosing to remain celibate. Yet such a decision is still regarded with
skepticism in a culture that caters to nuclear families. Rampant
divorce notwithstanding, families headed by married heterosex-
uals have somehow endured as a symbol of normality and enti-
tlement.

If there is a low-grade societal bias against people who don't
marry, it is certainly directed more at women than men. Eternal
bachelors may spark curiosity, but they also enjoy a kind of rak-
ish mystique. Not so the aging unmarried, childless woman who
is usually pitied, the assumption being that no one wanted her.
Either that or she is simply too selfish and self-absorbed to share
herself with a husband and children—the implication being that
she disdains the traditional woman's role, which has always
revolved around the perpetuation of the species. The skepticism
goes a level deeper with nuns, who renounce sex along with the
husband and the offspring. While some people bluntly assume
that many women become nuns because they, too, lacked options
in the so-called real world, surely no one believes that describes
every nun. Which means that there are some women out there

who rushed to embrace a very hard life, having rejected what is on offer in ours.

But how could they possibly? some laypeople wonder. What quickens their pulse if not the promise of a romance or sexual encounter, a husband and children sometime thereafter? To so many outsiders, the nun's personal life, such as it is, looks shapeless and empty. But they fail to realize that the feeling goes both ways. In the book *The Nuns*, on the subject of "human things like marriage and motherhood," one sister says, "It's a joy if you're meant to have them, and dust and ashes if you're not."

Still, choosing a stripped-down life will always be mystifying in a culture that enables the naked strivings of entertainers, politicians, and showboaters like Donald Trump. A generalization to be sure, but we tend not to celebrate the circumspect self-deniers—as if moderation and contentment were somehow un-American. Ours is also a culture that encourages endless hours in gyms and on treadmills, so fervent is our belief in self-improvement and physical beauty. For some people, especially those in cosmopolitan cities, how curious it is to find women whose disregard for vanity has allowed them to gain weight and dress downright unfashionably.

Perhaps because our culture is still so young, we hanker like adolescents for constant titillation, judging from our furious promulgation and consumption of sexual images in movies, newspapers, magazines, and on television. From the lewd monologues of late-night talk-show hosts to commonplace "parental advisory" stickers on rap and rock CDs to the detailed coverage of the president's sordid sexual transgressions, we are all so steeped in sexuality that to say no to the self-gratifying realm of sex is to go sharply against the grain. People in this society who choose a celibate life take a bold and lonely stand—and invite a sometimes hostile kind of curiosity.

So mysterious is the notion of voluntary celibacy that some assume only an eccentric would embrace it. Hence the wild and widespread presumptions regarding the typical nun's true nature: Either she is an angel on earth or an embittered old prune obsessed with sex, who vents her frustration by beating up on schoolchildren. Evidence of these extremes is plentiful in the popular culture, for which nuns have served as unhappy fodder for years. The novelty items—the T-shirts, wind-up toys such as "Nunzilla," the popular hand puppet known as the "Boxing Nun"—tend to depict them as ghouls and pugilists. Meanwhile, "good" nuns as pictured in the "Warrior Nun" comic books are chesty avengers in slit skirts and thigh-high boots. In our experience of nuns, sex is never far from our minds. The British nun Sister Wendy Beckett has achieved cult status with her written and televised art-history tours that occasionally find her pointing out the "lovely and fluffy" pubic hair on a Stanley Spencer nude or the shapely buttocks in a pool scene by David Hockney or the technical achievement of *The Bather of Valpinçon*: "From the long neck right down to the cleave of the buttocks, it's as though Ingres has licked his paint adoringly over every part of her!" Quite possibly the popularity of Sister Wendy owes at least a little to the thrill of hearing a hermitic nun talk dirty.

The question of nuns' sexuality—or presumed lack of it—has informed any number of strange portrayals in the movies. Traditionally, movies have great difficulty imagining nuns as sentient, integrated adults, so sidetracked are the filmmakers by the fact of their chastity. Often movie nuns are paragons of purity, absurdly unsullied by life on earth. *Come to the Stable* (1949) opens with

Celeste Holm and Loretta Young gliding about in habits on what looks like a snowy moonscape, and soon enough they are behaving as though they are from another planet as well. Placid and one-dimensional, they reduce everyone they encounter to deferential ninnies. It is difficult to imagine the women as former girls with parents, a home, a history. At best, intimations of a prior life are telegraphed decorously on-screen, as in the 1945 movie *The Bells of St. Mary's* when Ingrid Bergman's sister superior is counseling a young girl against considering religious life too hastily. She needs to experience life first, she says—football games, proms, parties and . . . other things before she can really know if this is the life for her. As she gazes off luminously, the nun seems to be recalling a sweet but distant romance from her own past. It is an honest moment in an otherwise implausible confection.

While the pure and pious nuns of film seem to have been magically relieved of all human urges, movie nuns at the other end of the spectrum tend to be cast as sexual hysterics—women fixated on the sex they aren't allowed to have. In *Black Narcissus* (1946), the story of five nuns sent to establish a mountaintop convent in the Himalayas, one nun is so undone by the heat, the dust, and the piercing gaze of a shorts-wearing British local, she steals about the convent like a wild animal, the whites of her eyes glinting in the shadows. Ultimately she plunges to her death following a mad struggle with the sister superior, who happens to be sexually frustrated also. At least this movie is visually sumptuous and heartfelt—a far cry from the wretched *The Devils* (1971), in which Vanessa Redgrave plays a humpbacked mother superior who works herself into a sexual frenzy fantasizing about Christ as she shuffles along on her knees murmuring the sorrowful mysteries and gouging her palms bloody with a crucifix.

There is also a common tendency in the movies to infantalize nuns. Often they are shown as giggling naïfs, as in *Lilies of the Field* (1963), where the nuns literally cluster and titter when their guest (Sidney Poitier) brings them lollipops, of all things, from the store. Here it seems that celibacy is tantamount to childishness. Elsewhere a puerile innocence masks a wanton excitability, as if the nuns, given half a chance, would gorge themselves on sensuality: The unlikely sisters of 1992's *Sister Act* go drastically from shut-ins to thrill-seekers in the course of the movie, all because a randy nightclub singer has shown up and given them license.

The image of nuns as closet sybarites is played out blatantly in *Two Mules for Sister Sara* (1970), in which a gunslinger (Clint Eastwood) is improbably allied with a nun he's just met (she's half dressed and about to be raped when he fortuitously happens by). Would-be hilarity ensues as Eastwood attempts to control his libido during their misadventures that follow ("I'll say one thing, Sister, I sure would like to have met up with you before you took to them clothes and them vows"). The joke of the movie comes at the end, when the nun, played prissily by Shirley MacLaine, rips off her veil and reveals her true identity as a saucy, lovable prostitute. Of course, now the gunslinger is in quite a rush to finally have sex with her, and not only because he has grown so frustrated. One senses an archetypal male fantasy at work—namely, that beneath school uniforms, virginal bridal gowns, and, yes, nuns' habits, there beats the heart of a whore.

Such depictions are what make a movie like 1995's *Dead Man Walking* a revelation. Counseling a death-row inmate who is flirtatious and predatory by turns, Susan Sarandon's Sister Helen Prejean illustrates the perfectly subversive notion that a nun can be strong, savvy, attractive, *and* vowed.

*   *   *

The inherent drama of the vow of chastity is underscored by the very sensuality of Catholicism, which, like romance, relies heavily on music, incense, candles, even wine. At one point during an Easter service in the chapel at the University of the Incarnate Word in San Antonio, the parishioners were invited to participate in a ritual in which they'd wash one another's feet, thereby emulating Christ's washing the feet of the Apostles the night before His Crucifixion. I was taken aback when the woman sitting next to me in the pew suddenly began removing her shoes, pulling up her slacks, and rolling down her nylon knee-highs. Parishioners throughout the church proceeded to the altar, sat down, and allowed another parishioner to wash, rub, and towel their feet while the choir surged.

Given the church's repressive attitude toward sexuality (forbidding premarital sex, unilaterally condemning homosexual acts), its perpetuation of earthy, sensual rites and customs, especially in religious life, seems incongruous. Such customs include frequent, pro forma kissing—of vestments, rings, statues, crucifixes, the floor, feet occasionally, and each other (the frequently tendered "kiss of peace"). At the Women's Ordination Conference in 1995, attended by several hundred nuns and others, there was an elaborate bread-breaking ritual at the dinner on the final night. At tables of eight or ten, different breads representing the cultures of the world—challah, pita bread, tortillas, and so on—were passed and blessed and blessed and passed; once it was time to actually eat a piece, it was moist and warm from everyone else's hand sweat. On each table was a carafe of rosé and a carafe of cranberry juice, chosen to approximate the color of the wine, which itself approximates the color of blood. Water, juice, and wine all were drunk from communal cups. The uninhibited ceremony seemed a bold antidote to the pre–Vatican II days when nuns weren't even supposed to touch one another. Yet even then the body of Christ was ecstatically ingested—the priest placing the host on a wet tongue in an open mouth. For the wide-eyed outsider this custom always sounded vaguely cannibalistic—never mind the purity and piety of those who avidly and regularly partook.

Many a pre–Vatican II convent seemed to encourage a relationship with Christ that bordered on the romantic in its fervor and exclusivity, promoting the idea that nuns are actually married to Christ. In her memoir, *Nun,* Mary Gilligan Wong describes a Valentine's Day custom in convent school where a junior is chosen to represent all the students as "Jesus's valentine sweetheart: She dresses in a long white gown and, announced by trumpets and surrounded by attendants, processes into the refectory to take her place of honor next to a red-robed Little King statue." Before the taking of vows, notepaper was placed on a desk in the study hall on which the girls wrote love notes to Jesus; then they tucked them in their bras on the day of the ceremony. In most orders, women entering the novitiate actually walked down the aisle in wedding dresses and veils. On the day of her final profession the sister would receive a ring that was practically indistinguishable from a wedding band.

But nothing could communicate the romantic dimension of religious life more vividly than the Bernini sculpture of St. Teresa of Ávila depicting one of her recurring visions. The overwrought marble shows an angel lifting her habit and thrusting a golden spear toward her heart as Teresa seems to swoon, her lounging form both weak and welcoming. In her autobiography, St. Teresa describes the moment of penetration and its rapturous aftermath, which left her feeling "totally inflamed with a great love for

God": "The sweetness of this intense pain is so extreme, there is no wanting it to end, and the soul is not satisfied with anything less than God."

Yet while nuns were cast in the role of Christ's wife and lover before Vatican II, the subject of sex was studiously avoided. "The attitude could be summed up by the instruction we received in the novitiate from our director when we were talking about the vows of poverty, chastity, and obedience," says Sister Jeannine Gramick, a School Sister of Notre Dame who until recently co-ran a ministry aimed at increasing sensitivity toward lesbians and gays. "We spent days, maybe a good month, discussing the vow of poverty. Then, for the vow of chastity, we were given three lectures on human reproduction, all of which we knew from high school anyway. And after those three lectures we were told, 'There is nothing forbidden by the vow of chastity that isn't already forbidden by the sixth and the ninth commandments [which denounce adultery and coveting thy neighbor's wife, respectively], so now we're going to go on to the vow of obedience.' We never discussed feelings, orientation, desire."

In the crudest manner sex was stamped out, beginning with the way the women were expected to look. Some wore figure-flattening undergarments, while others sheared their locks and shaved their heads, arguably a highly symbolic repudiation—hair being so closely associated with feminine allure. Often nuns were instructed to dress and undress beneath their nightgowns so there would be no stray glimpses of their own nakedness. Meanwhile, men—the lay variety, especially—were portrayed as nefarious temptations. "You weren't to have any dealings with men," says Sister Jeannine. "Or at least you were supposed to minimize your dealings, your conversation and contact. For example, if you were in a car and a man was driving, you were to sit in the backseat, even if there were only two of you in the car." Nuns were never supposed to look into the eyes of a man, which caused great anxiety during visits from the optometrist. One nun almost collapsed from the stress of having to hold her eyes open and stare for several seconds while the doctor administered eyedrops.

Yet the reasoning behind such rules was never discussed. As a result, nuns feeling frustrated or confused by the vow of chastity had scant internal resources to draw on and no one to turn to. The ill-informed nun experiencing an urge or a sense of loss with regard to her sexuality often felt that she was being disloyal to Christ. How was she to know this was only natural? She couldn't possibly, given the church's forbidding attitude, vividly expressed in *Sacra Virginitas*, Pope Pius XII's 1954 encyclical on consecrated virginity. As the pope stated, virginity requires "a constant vigilance and struggle to contain and dominate rebellious movements of body and soul, a flight from the importunings of this world, a struggle to conquer the wiles of Satan." Rather than explore such a putatively dark and destructive realm, the nun was encouraged to sublimate her emotions, scrubbing floors and dishes and clothes and tending furiously to her ministry by way of compulsive compensation. One former cloistered nun would routinely lose herself in the endless labor of farming. She was grateful for the outlet. "You have to have outside work!" the former nun says. "You have to get away from the temptations of your own body. You have to work it out somehow."

Before Vatican II there was also the thorny business of penitential practices that involved medieval paraphernalia: chain girdles, studded metal bands worn around arms and legs, a crucifix full of nails worn against the skin, hair shirts, and a twelve-inch cord with knotted tips called a "discipline," with which a nun whipped herself into a state of abject humility while supposedly subduing carnal urges and bodily inclinations. Typically nuns were told by their superiors that the use of such equipment wasn't intended to cause serious pain or injury. These were, on the whole, symbolic exercises through which the nun could share in Christ's suffering and offer up her own pain for the sins of humankind. Still, in that cold, quiet moment when the nun knelt in her cell, discipline in hand, she was on her own, dealing with the chaotic and contradictory emotions that this macabre custom inevitably provoked.

But airing her ambivalence about the practice was as difficult as being stoic. During Vatican II community meetings in which customs were scrutinized, the issue of self-flagellation sometimes arose. The sisters in one very traditional, contemplative community were accustomed to retreating to their cells once a week, taking down the tops of their robes, and beating their bare torsos with the discipline for the duration of a psalm. Then a bell would ring, after which the sisters quickly showered, reassembled their habits, and went back to work. During a communitywide discussion of the practice, one sister was bold and honest enough to suggest that for her it was quite counterproductive: Rather than subduing her, she found the beatings somewhat arousing, reminding her that she actually had breasts, which in another life could have nursed a baby or given her sexual pleasure. The dilemma was more than the community's superior could handle. The topic was hastily dropped, while the mortified sister was left to wrestle privately with her confusion and shame. Few communities encourage the use of the discipline anymore—which isn't to suggest that the vowed woman's struggle with the temptation of sexuality is in any way a thing of the past.

* * *

Often laypeople become unwitting celibates. Perhaps they have been in a relationship for years and the nature of the bond changed—the sex just went away, and they can live with that. Today there are large numbers of sophisticated urban women in their forties and fifties who certainly never said, "Under no circumstances will I marry or have children"; it simply turned out that way. Life takes unanticipated twists and turns, but rarely are grand declarations made about such things as one's current and future sexual status.

The idea of a woman boldly and publicly giving up sex is what makes the vow of chastity so difficult for laypeople to fathom. It is surprising, then, to find out that nuns, too, occasionally grow into a permanently celibate state over time. Even if they were completely sincere when they took the vow, its practical reality manifested gradually and unconsciously. "I didn't say to myself, 'I don't want children.' I did," says Dominican sister Joan McVeigh. "I had a guy I'd been going with for quite a while. We even talked about having as many children as we had to have to build a basketball team—both of us were crazy about basketball. When you're seventeen, you're stupid; you think about things like that." She chuckles at the thought. "I didn't say, 'Well, I'm giving up this and going to that. I'm doing this for God; I'm sacrificing. I'll never have children, and I can't marry Johnny.' It never occurred to me."

Some nuns are unmarried, chaste, and childless because it so clearly and naturally suits their vocation. They travel widely and give themselves over to the needs of others. Being celibate makes life as they know it possible. "I don't think I ever said, 'I'm going to give this up,' " Maryknoll sister Mary Lou Daoust says of marriage, sex, and children. "Rather, I chose another alternative for myself about how I wanted to live my life. And in so choosing I've been incredibly gifted with friends and experience, so I can't ever really even think of life in terms of 'I gave up this in order to get that.' " Asked if she has ever wondered what a more conventional life might have been like for her, Sister Mary Lou responds, "Not really. I'm kind of a pragmatist. You make your choices. And certainly I had the opportunity to get married. But I've not really been into looking back and wondering. My choices work for me."

Many nuns would say their life is simply too consuming for intimate relations and family. If one is wholeheartedly honoring her vocation, she must give it everything she has got. She cannot be reserving a piece of herself for a lover or a mate later in the day. In *Sacra Virginitas,* Pius XII wrote,

> How, for example, could a missionary such as the wonderful St. Francis Xavier, a father of the poor such as the merciful St. Vincent de Paul, a zealous educator of youth like St. John Bosco, a tireless "mother of emigrants" like St. Francis Xavier Cabrini, have accomplished such gigantic and painful labors, if each had to look after the corporal and spiritual needs of a wife or husband and children?

To live happily in such a focused, committed life is to appreciate the idea that the vows don't rein in the nun so much as they liberate her. It is a notion that's as old as Christianity itself. In her discussion of the women of the Roman Empire, Jo Ann McNamara writes in *Sisters in Arms,* "The single concept that appears to have attracted all the active religious women was the power of celibacy to free them from the disabilities of womanhood," numbering among those "the long captivity of pregnancy." Although the physical perils of childbirth are no longer quite as grave, there is much in the contemporary woman's lot that could be considered disabling, given the incalculable sacrifices that child-rearing requires. Just as the vow of poverty prevents a hobbling attachment to acquisitions (and mortgages and credit-card payments), the vow of chastity relieves a woman of the child-care burden and frees her from the shackles of possessive exclusivity. There is no husband to rush home to, no sick child to attend to, no closing of ranks and retreating at various points throughout the day, in the custom of typical American families. She is available. As one very busy nun committed to social justice on an international level puts it, "I can do what I do because I have nothing to lose."

When one ponders the seriousness of the vow of chastity, it is worth considering whether the married woman's vows are all that much easier to keep. Aren't there regular temptations, and doesn't she have to reexamine her vows continually? One nun says that being celibate isn't so different from being monogamously married in that you don't wake up every day thinking, "God, I hope I'm faithful today"—it just isn't as dramatic as all that. But what is easy for one person might be a great hardship for the next. An elderly nun marvels at the lengths some secular women go to in order to look attractive, at least partly for the benefit of potential mates. Running, working out, and shopping for makeup and clothes—now, *that's* sacrificing, the nun says with a slow shake of her head.

While there seems to be something frighteningly absolute about the vow of chastity, some women religious have found ways to express themselves uniquely within the strict confines of

the vow. In her small cell at the Maryknoll motherhouse in Ossi-
ning, New York, Sister Jean Pruitt has kept a smattering of
mementos—some peacock feathers, dried roses, and candles.
The place feels like a dorm room, headquarters for someone who
is on the move and adept at traveling light. She has also pinned
up photos: Jean as a young woman with her biological family,
and with the children she informally adopted in her mission territory of Tanzania, where the distinction is made between the
mama mzazi—"the mother who bore me," and the *mama mlezi*—
"the mother who raised me." Sister Jean is the *mama mlezi* to
three boys and two girls. Given the cooperative spirit of child
rearing in Tanzania, Sister Jean has plenty of supervision for her
charges when she is required to travel, as is so often the case.

Now sixty, Sister Jean has spent twenty-six of the last thirty
years there, helping the young and the disabled make batiks,
leather goods, and jewelry in the renowned handicraft cooperative that she cofounded. She has also pioneered nutritional and
educational services, arranging for some young Tanzanians
schooling that would be an unattainable luxury without her help
and connections. A few years ago one of her own "daughters"
won a full scholarship to Smith College, the 1905 alma mater of
Mary Josephine Rogers, who founded the Maryknoll Sisters in
1912.

In a few days, Sister Jean will be returning to Africa, having
just completed the domestic complement of her role in the order,
a stint in the communications office at the motherhouse. On the
wall a few feet away is a constant reminder of the life's harsher
side: a large portrait of the four churchwomen, including two
Maryknoll sisters, who were murdered by Salvadoran National
Guardsmen in 1980. This afternoon Sister Jean is describing the

time in 1993 that she and a Benedictine father organized a fifty-
kilometer trek from Tanzania over the border into Mozambique.
During the recent war between FRELIMO (the Front for the Lib-
eration of Mozambique) and RENAMO (the Mozambican
National Resistance), the border had become a site of relentless
bombing and fighting as hundreds of thousands of Mozambicans
sought sanctuary in Tanzania and elsewhere. The trek was a
show of support and solidarity. The thirty-three marchers, comprised of some religious and a church youth group, set out at five
o'clock in the morning. "We had to do it all in one day because
it's a game reserve," Sister Jean says. "There are wild animals
and no place to stay along the way, so you just have to hope you
make it before the sun sets." After taking canoes across the mile-
wide Ruvuma River, they began to walk through the forest in the
ninety-degree heat, singing songs for strength along the way. But
by noon they had run out of water. Eventually the group found a
bog and filled up their containers with a buggy liquid the color of
tea. It was only one of two brief stops they dared take.

At a certain point Sister Jean started to feel severe pain in her
feet, and she fell behind. Her "son" Lusungu, who was fourteen
at the time and marching alongside her, whispered, "You've been
leading, and you have to continue." It was all Sister Jean needed
to pick up the pace. Eventually they stumbled into Palma,
Mozambique, at 6:30 P.M., just as the sun was setting. By the time
the marchers arrived, thousands of villagers had gathered to
cheer and greet them with hymns. As she describes the epic day,
Sister Jean fondles a dried-out mahogany-hued pod nearly as
long as the jawbone of a horse, which she'd found on the ground
while they were marching. She took it with her, as a memento. It
was, after all, the most wonderful journey—even though she had
to have two toenails surgically removed when she got back.

It is a different life, with its intense and unrelenting flow of service, love and energy outward—toward the Tanzanians in Sister Jean's case, as well as to the sisters at the motherhouse on the other side of the world. It is also, frequently, a dangerous life, impossible for someone with conventionally familial or sexual attachments. As I listen to Sister Jean's story, the details of her youth are playing in my head, especially the fact that she was working at the Automobile Club of Southern California just before coming to Maryknoll. In honoring her vows, Sister Jean has sacrificed. But she has also been extravagantly rewarded.

While intimate relations just aren't viable for many sisters, reasons for honoring the vow of chastity go deeper. One has to transcend the self-centered, self-pleasuring precinct of sex in order to dwell fully in the realm of the spirit. When a nun lives the celibate, chaste life, carnal immediacy and particularity give way to a more expansive way of loving. Some nuns have such a lively, sharp-eyed, open way about them, their capacity for undiluted focus on whomever they are with can only be described as sexy.

Discussing celibate chastity, nuns often talk in a basic way about energy. In the best of worlds they can creatively reroute untapped sexual energy into their work and also their prayer (one vocal version of which is called "ejaculatory"). Just as some sleeplessness and a certain degree of hunger can refine the senses, abstaining from sex can intensify one's interaction with the world, and especially one's focus on God. Hence the ecstatic dimension of prayer for those who take it and practice it very seriously. Such nuns are quick to say that their own sexuality hasn't dried up and disappeared; in fact, having sexual feelings often enhances the sacrifice. It is easy to give up things that never mattered. Sermonizing about the perpetual desire to know Christ and the earthly sacrifices that such a mission requires, one priest described the nun's life as "one long, long yearning."

Sister Diana, a thirty-three-year-old cloistered nun, says that lately she's been feeling the absence of sexuality in her life more acutely than usual. She is keenly aware of the attractive workmen who come often to the monastery to do repairs. And her relationship with a seminarian with whom she corresponds seems to be deepening. They love each other and talk about everything, including the sense of sexual longing they both sometimes feel. Sister Diana claims not to be troubled by this at all. "The joy of being in your thirties!" She laughs, gently refuting the common misconception that cloistered nuns are somehow immune to the hormonal ebb and flow. "I can't do anything about it except to be with it," Sister Diana says, "remembering, with a smile, to thank God that everything is in working order, accepting this potential as a gift made more precious because it is consecrated to Him, reserved for His designs." She has found ways to appreciate the carnal pull; it is then, as she says, that she can really "taste the vow."

This isn't the first time that Sister Diana's devotion to religious life has been tested, which might seem strange for someone whose path appeared so unobstructed for so long. Growing up in Bayonne, New Jersey, Diana reveled in Catholic pageantry. This, for her, was where romance resided. Her family went to Mass every Sunday in a church that was a marvel of stained glass, paintings, and frescoes; Diana entertained herself for hours staring at the four evangelists gathered around a ceiling fixture. There was a tomb in one of the church's side altars featuring a life-size statue of a lifeless Christ. On Holy Saturday the tomb was decorated with pots of flowers brought in by the schoolkids. Diana would plead with her mother for lilies on these occasions because Sister always put the lilies on top. At Christmas one of the side altars held a tableau of a manger scene. A few days after Christmas, Diana and her classmates would line up to kiss the statue of the infant Jesus, being held by one of the sisters. Thanks to her faith, Diana's life was orderly and exotically mysterious at once.

When she was in third grade, Diana was chosen to be a lector, one who does the readings at Mass. And she enthusiastically participated in the Forty Hours devotion to the Blessed Sacrament that took place during Lent. Wearing a small cape and a mantilla on her head, Diana was one of the children who processed behind the Blessed Sacrament, or body of Christ, in its ornate monstrance protected by a large brocade canopy held by four ushers. The old Polish ladies sitting in the pews serenaded them with somber hymns. Diana found herself swept up in the rituals, although never more so than on her First Communion, when the host was placed on her tongue for the first time in her life. Walking back to the pew, her hands folded perfectly, she knew that this was a spectacular thing—"that Jesus was inside of me!" as she remembers it. "So very close." At the time she felt a strange sort of pull.

The feeling deepened in fifth grade when she had to write a report on a saint for school. She had chosen St. Thérèse of Lisieux, the fervent nineteenth-century Carmelite nun also known as the Little Flower. St. Thérèse's autobiography, *The Story of a Soul*, came as a revelation to Diana. To crave, at age fifteen, a life of abject humility, simplicity, and service and not be dissuaded from that life by anything seemed so brilliant and brave. At a time when other girls were developing crushes on boys, Diana was transfixed by St. Thérèse's quiet passion. In fact, she began to realize that she, too, was destined to become a nun one day. "And I can be a very single-minded person," Sister Diana says now, laughing.

But just as another mother might forbid her teenage daughter to marry, Sister Diana's own mother tried to distract her from her future spouse: She insisted that Diana remain in parochial school and then go on to college. So with the calm ardor of a girl planning her elopement, Diana obeyed her mother's wishes.

Diana attended a small Catholic college in New Jersey, where she listened to her Gregorian-chant CDs while the rest of the campus thrummed with Duran Duran and Depeche Mode (which she appreciated also). And it was there, at the college bookstore, that she met Tom, a very all-American and boyish-looking man who was standing ahead of her in line. They started talking. It was the first of many deep and meandering conversations, during which they discovered a shared interest in the writings of Thomas Merton, among other things. One night when Tom saw Diana carrying around a breviary, he asked her if she wanted to become a nun. She swore Tom to secrecy and told him yes.

They became best friends, of the platonic variety; Diana's first love was Christ, after all. Yet in a completely unprecedented way, she was experiencing feelings that could only be described as chaotic *and* erotic. "I wanted to become a nun, and nuns don't fall in love," Sister Diana says. "So when I did, it was just a total shock." Never the type to take her passions lightly, Diana decided that Tom needed to know. So one day she pulled him into the chapel, of all places, and bared her heart.

Maybe because Tom knew that Diana was bound for the monastery, and maybe because he had sexual feelings for her as well, he didn't accept the information gracefully. He started to avoid her—actually walking the other way if he saw her coming. Diana was confused and devastated. What followed was a grim round of discussions, weak explanations, and unsatisfying apologies.

Looking back, Diana regards the experience as a critical step on the road to religious life: It was the first time she'd experienced unconditional love—the kind that brings you out of yourself almost physically. "One of my retreat masters asked me if I had ever fallen in love," she remembers. "When I told him I had, he said, 'That's good. Because otherwise you probably would have fallen in love with someone in the monastery. And having had that experience will help you grow.' I've never acted so unselfishly toward anyone as I did toward Tom, and I think that's how I should love the Lord. The experience was agony, of course, but I'm glad I went through it."

Suppose Tom had returned her affections with full force. Is it possible that everything would have turned out differently? Sister Diana seems especially vulnerable to such questions, as there is so much of the secular girl still present in her smile, her spiky laugh, and her lavishly detailed descriptions of her lusty schoolgirl crush. But she suddenly grows placid and somewhat remote when she says that her dream of becoming a nun had at no time been threatened. Feelings for a man were simply a testament to the confusing richness of life, as well as to the reality that becoming a nun would require sacrifice. As for Tom, "He's married now," Sister Diana says matter-of-factly. "He's happily vowed, and I'm happily vowed," Ultimately they were able to resume their friendship. Tom even attended Sister Diana's final profession, with his wife and baby girl.

Just like a married woman whose problems, weaknesses, and temptations don't disappear the day she pledges vows, Sister Diana might always struggle with celibacy. Since becoming a nun, the time she missed the company of men the most was when her father died one week before she took her final vows. As she grieved, her desire to be hugged by a man was almost primal. "There are times of struggle—the loneliness, the ache of wanting to be held, knowing that my womb will never carry a child, that I will never experience the intimacy of intercourse," Sister Diana says. "But it makes the gift of myself all the more poignant and precious. I don't feel deprived or thwarted in accepting His call to be entirely His. This life agrees with me," Sister Diana says. "It is a fit."

That a cloistered nun like Sister Diana could speak so freely about such things is proof of how much has changed since Vatican II. Dovetailing as it did with the women's movement and the widespread encouragement of self-expression, Vatican II gave rise to a great sharing and plumbing of emotions in many convents, while redefining sexual urges as something completely natural. Suddenly nonsexual touch—hugs and kisses—between nuns was considered very acceptable, as was the supportive touching of laypeople. Not only could a nun's hug easily be considered a tool in her ministry, it was finally acknowledged that she herself needed to be wrapped in loving arms from time to time. She also had to exercise and eat right, now that it had been widely agreed upon that nuns actually had bodies as well as souls. That healthy, well-rounded, self-aware, affectionate women made better nuns was an idea that was at long last gaining strength.

Yet such revolutionary attitudes contributed in no small way to the great exodus from the convents. Now that lay life, marriage, and motherhood were no longer seen as a lesser calling, it suddenly was that much easier to leave. In addition, many a post–Vatican II sister found herself working closely with men, which enhanced the chances of falling in love (a nursing sister's leaving the convent to marry a doctor she worked with was becoming an increasingly common phenomenon). As the gap between religious life and lay life narrowed, the leap into marriage no longer seemed so drastic. At one point I interviewed a nun in her forties who wore fashionable business suits and held an editorial position in a busy newsroom. She was unrecognizable as a nun, by either her appearance or her work. After our first meeting I called her a few times with follow-up questions, but she never called back. A year or so later I was shocked but not surprised to read her wedding announcement in the newspaper.

This liberating new way of thinking about nuns' sexuality prompted any number of sisters to acknowledge their own latent, erotic urges and, in some cases, the desire to act upon them. Many among them who still wanted to remain in religious life attempted tortured reinterpretations of the vow that might allow for some sexual experimentation. Already obedience was rightly being reimagined as obedience to one's conscience as opposed to one's superior or the Vatican; now chastity was being reconceived in some corners as a willingness to love nonexclusively—yet love nonetheless. For one cheerful, athletic young postulant, celibacy was by far the most difficult part of religious life, a vow that is heeded and renewed one day at a time. "I like men!" she'd say helplessly, with a laugh. On occasion she even wondered if discreet sexual relations and religious life couldn't be reconciled. As the postulant saw it, God wouldn't want His nuns frustrated and embittered. Maybe not. Yet it was somehow not surprising to learn that this particular postulant gave up the life before making final vows.

Nuns of the old school disdain any sort of creative tinkering with the vows. They argue that this existence was never intended to be easy or convenient. "What's the point of religious life?" Mother Hildegard asks. "To just go off and do what you want to do? Fine, do it, but don't call it religious life."

For Mother Hildegard, as for so many nuns, not only is it unthinkable to have sex as a religious, she has never had sex at all. Of course, premarital sex was less common in her day. "Nice girls just didn't do it," she says. That she is a virgin clearly is a point of pride for Mother Hildegard. She seems slightly uncomfortable with the number of nonvirgins—the older women, the divorcées and widows—who become nuns these days. But on some level she has accepted that as a condition of modern religious life. As she says, "It used to be on your profession day you had what was called the consecration of the virgin"—a long ritual full of ancient prayers, presided over by a bishop or an abbot, during which the virgins were crowned with a wreath of synthetic flowers that they would be buried with. "Well, today we have no doubt in our minds that some young women entering aren't virgins. So now basically what we say is, it's the life after vows" that matters, and that has to be celibate and chaste.

Mother Hildegard says that she had many romantic opportunities in secular life. "I lived in Hawaii and Germany for a couple of years, fell in love with a young man in Switzerland whose father was a marquis," she says unsentimentally. "In college I was engaged to a medical student. But I'd known since I was fourteen that I wanted to be a nun, so I just had to make a decision. And I regretted it many times. In fact, when I was in the novitiate, I used to say, 'Oh, my God, to think I gave up Sergio for this!'—that was kind of my theme song. The community would tease me about it. But since final vows it's been 'This is what it is, and this is where I'm supposed to be.' "When asked if celibacy is ever difficult, Mother Hildegard says, "I think I've always taken my relationship with Christ very seriously. For me that was the ultimate romance. So I can't say I missed it. I wouldn't be human if I didn't to a degree miss having kids, yet I very seriously feel that I am the mother to Christ's children in the church. I mean, I've got more kids than most women out there. And I really believe that."

She is quick to point out that celibacy doesn't keep one from taking pleasure in men. For instance, she has met all kinds of wonderful men through her farming work and classes. "I think I have more relationships with men now than most married women," she says. "We have great working relationships, and I thoroughly enjoy them." Furthermore, her crush on Peter Jennings runs deep. "He's our absolute favorite," she says. "I mean, isn't he just the sexiest man in America?"

It is a coarse and common assumption among a certain kind of man that women who reject their advances must be lesbians. That is a self-protective, macho rationale: If she doesn't want me, she must not like men at all. There is a trace of that thinking in the prevalent assumption that most nuns—having turned their back on marriage and motherhood—are lesbians as well. Either that or they are dangerous flouters of the status quo. For certain people the lesbian explanation is vastly more tenable than the explosive idea of a heterosexual woman's choosing to devote herself to something other than a man.

Sister Jeannine Gramick, who has done studies and counseled lesbian nuns, estimates that fewer than 7 percent of nuns are lesbian, which is comparable to the number of lesbians in lay life. (Sister Jeannine acknowledges that the nun figure might be underreported, at least partly because sisters could be out of touch with this side of themselves and because they tend to be private about such things.) Of course, the existence of lesbian nuns makes a certain degree of plain sense: The convent may have exerted its own special pull for women who prefer the company of other women, whether or not they were even aware of their own sexual bent at the time. For them the convent was less a strict world of sacrifice than a kind of Shangri-la, despite regular warnings about "particular friendships," or "PFs": One wasn't supposed to single out another nun for her affections, as that would undermine community and one's own commitment to the Lord. As such, nuns were expected to recreate in groups of three or more, and they were never allowed in one another's cells. There was something unexplained and tantalizing about the taboo of PFs. The book *The Nuns* quotes the *Carmelite Manual for Novices on the Cultivation of Chastity*:

> Touch no one, and do not allow yourself to be touched by anyone without necessity or evident reason, however innocent. Repress and fly from as a mortal plague, even though spiritual in their origin, particular friendships and familiar conversations arising from an attractive appearance, pleasing manner, or an agreeable disposition.

Eventually many sisters realized that "PFs" was probably a veiled reference to lesbianism.

"When I went into the convent, I think I really felt that I had a calling, I really believe that," says Jean O'Leary, a lesbian who was a sister from 1966 to 1971. A drummer in a band who'd once been suspended for putting goldfish in the holy-water font at her Midwestern parochial school, Jean was fun, well liked, and not without male suitors. But dating and marrying didn't interest her. Convent life did. "In retrospect I think what I really wanted was to be on an island of all women. That had been one of my fantasies growing up—to live in a world where you can actually be gay and have dates and do things that normal people do. And there was no place like that back in those days. Unconsciously, that was one of the main reasons I chose to go into the convent."

Jean's Pennsylvania convent was situated near woods and a lake. It was a serene, remote place where relationships had a chance to flourish and intensify. Eventually Jean and another sister began stealing time together. One evening she and the sister were alone in a classroom when the chimes began to ring for vespers. Rather than report to chapel, they stayed where they were. As they stared at one another, motionless, the other sister reached out and began giving Jean a back rub. Jean pulled her gently to the seat beside her. In the rumbling silence of vespers, they shared a kiss.

During their daily labors, using the excuse that they were going out to have a cigarette (disapproved of but never legislated against), they hugged and kissed. They also climbed into bed together after the lights were turned out. The bed was one of several in a dormitory-style room, with only a hanging sheet separating one from the next. "It wasn't like we did a lot of real unusual positions," Jean says. "It was just pretty simple, straightforward kind of stuff. I had the quietest orgasms I ever had in my life!" One day the sheets were taken down in a move that was intended to be progressive, allowing the sisters all to dress in each other's company. "But I was devastated," Jean says with a laugh.

In time Jean was juggling a few relationships, sneaking around and trying to minimize hurt feelings. She found her way regularly to the bed of one sister on the pretext of leaving a holy card on her end table. Sisters often left holy cards for one another with messages written on the back, such as "Thank you, Sister, for a wonderful day." In Jean's case the custom gave her entrée onto a floor where she normally would not be allowed, as her lover was a year ahead of her at the convent.

As convoluted as the machinations eventually became, the strangest part was that at no time did Jean and her lovers talk about what was going on. The words "gay" and "lesbian" were never uttered, and in the clear light of day, amid their routines and spiritual obligations, the sisters' capacity for denial was powerful. "Although it was a huge part of my life," Jean says—"I mean, I lived for those women and being with them and being intimate—but it was something you could sort of pretend wasn't happening." Matters weren't helped when Jean confessed to a priest that she thought she might be homosexual (she still couldn't bring herself to utter the even more perverse-sounding "lesbian"). "And he basically told me I wasn't," Jean remembers. "He said, 'You're perfectly normal. Your hormones are raging, and this just happens to be the environment you're in, so this is how it's getting expressed.' And I remember feeling more lonely at that time than I ever had in my life."

The entire convent was complicit in the denial, or so it seemed. One day when Jean and another sister were walking by the lake, holding hands and kissing, the novice mistress summoned them. She told them to stop because walking by the lake was against the rules—nothing more, despite her obvious knowledge of what was going on. Things took a decidedly farcical turn on another day, when everyone was in the recreation room and the postulant mistress, who was putting together a mosaic, asked Jean to fetch her some more tiles from the laundry. Jean asked if another sister could accompany her—a sister with whom she was having a relationship. Reluctantly, the postulant mistress agreed. Once in the dark of the laundry, the two sisters gave in to their passion. Suddenly the room filled with cold, hard light. The postulant mistress was standing in the doorway staring at the two sisters, whose headdresses were off.

Jean was horrified; she was sure that the next day would be her last at the convent. In no way was she prepared for what would happen as she stood before the postulant mistress in her office the following morning. Rather than reprimand her, the postulant mistress said, "The least you could have done was talk to me." Her meaning was clear: She was jealous. Soon after, she and Jean struck up a physical relationship as well.

Regardless of how it may sound, Jean says she doesn't think the convent was "a hotbed of lesbianism"—she had simply found her way into the vortex of some particularly like-minded sisters. And despite Jean's own avidity, the guilt overrode the pleasures whenever she allowed herself to think about what she was doing. "For a while I tried to justify it by thinking, 'Couldn't we interpret the vow to mean that we have enough love to go around to everyone—a universal love instead of a negative chastity kind of thing?' But towards the end I told myself, 'Okay, Jean, face this, you really are gay'—I *still* couldn't say lesbian. I felt I had to get out into the world and figure it out, or at least get out of the convent, because it was becoming too ridiculous."

Now Jean is a Los Angeles businesswoman who has also worked as a gay-rights activist. All these years later she is still ambivalent about the vow of chastity and the sublimation that it requires. "The reasons given for chastity were that you were saving your love for God," she says. "And if your energy is directed to loving other people, you can't be focused on being the bride of

Christ and doing His work in the world. It's probably healthier to be well rounded, but a woman could get very distracted with a child at home with chicken pox or dyslexia or whatever. If she has a husband or lover and they are having a fight, that has an impact. On the other hand, that's life. Even if you're celibate, if you have friends, you can be affected by those emotions."

The guilt and the time-consuming intrigue notwithstanding, Jean finds it hard to argue for celibate chastity; as she remembers it, she was always in top spiritual form during those times when she was in love. And maybe she was a better, more openhearted person. But religious life requires considerably more. Any woman who has lived in community can vouch for the destructiveness of divided loyalties. As so many say, in a real community you can't have people pairing off. "[Being in love] energized me and gave me a lot more reason for living—for getting up in the morning," Jean says. "I've never felt happier than those times in the convent, living every moment to the fullest. It's like you smell the grass when you wake up and you see the sky and it's just a beautiful day. Those were idyllic days at the motherhouse. All your needs were taken care of, and all you've got to do is focus on . . . well, for me it was women."

If the lack of discussion before Vatican II contributed to the pressure of being celibate, imagine what lesbian nuns were going through. Not only were they suppressing sexual desires, they were hiding forbidden information about their orientation— from their sisters and from themselves in many cases. (Some nuns report a considerable degree of sub rosa homophobia in the convent, especially during the repressive pre–Vatican II days.) According to Sister Jeannine Gramick, "Frankly, it was presumed that everyone entered the community as a heterosexual, and then after you entered you were asexual, so there was no need to talk about sexuality."

But that changed when communities began easing restrictions on what sort of reading materials were permitted in the enclosure, what could be watched on television, and how far a sister could stray from the convent. "When people began to read what secular society had produced about sexuality," says Sister Jeannine, "they wondered, 'Well, if I've felt sexually attracted to a sister, does that mean I am lesbian?' " In addition, the nuns who weren't virgins—those who were older and who had perhaps been married—in a sense brought sexuality, or at least sexual awareness, into the convent in an unprecedented way. For veteran nuns, accepting that was a challenge. One lesbian sister remembers coming out to another sister a few decades her senior. After some angry discussion the older sister finally softened and gave the younger one a hug as she cried. "It's just so hard for me," she admitted. "It's so different from what I know." Recognizing this generational rub, an administrative sister with the Daughters of Charity says firmly, "I personally would not encourage lesbian sisters to advertise."

These days, according to Sister Jeannine, "the interpretation is that a wholesome sexuality [for sisters] still would not include sexual genital expression. But there is a recognition that people have sexual desires and needs that have to be discussed and channeled in an appropriate way. Somehow those needs have to be fulfilled: If you are a human being, you can't live without intimacy. Repressing that need could make for a kind of truncated person who is afraid of being touched. We need to be touched, we need to hug people, and sometimes we even need to kiss someone"—not lingeringly or passionately, of course.

With discussion and understanding came the radical possibility for lesbian nuns to actually live a celibate religious life without having to deny their sexual identities. But expressing this newfound self-awareness would not be automatic or easy.

Growing up in the Midwest in the fifties, Sister Patricia remembers her childhood revolving around the church in the most gratifying way. Her extended family attended the same church as well, and everyone was involved in the fund-raisers, the dinners, and the parish-related social life. On occasion they made a pilgrimage to the local monastery, where they walked the Stations of the Cross outdoors. The first time she did this, at the age of four, she turned a corner and practically bumped into two nuns in full habit. "They fussed all over us," she remembers. "My folks practically genuflected in front of them. I thought, 'I want to be like that.' That's a very strong memory."

In high school Patricia wasn't much interested in boys. "It never occurred to me that that was different from what most kids were experiencing. In my circle none of us really dated. We group-dated." And no one ever talked about anything as darkly exotic as homosexuality. "I grew up in an asexual culture. Homosexuality just wasn't on my radar screen." So when she entered religious life after college, the idea that she might be a lesbian never came up. "I'd never met lesbian women, never thought about it. I just thought I was a good sister because I really loved the other nuns. And I was always grateful that celibacy was never an issue. Obedience was, but celibacy wasn't."

While Sister Patricia was working on the East Coast as an advocate for low-wage laborers, she started spending time with a religious brother named Philip who was living in a mission in the next town over. One night while they were walking on the beach at sunset, he confessed his love for Sister Patricia, adding that he'd be willing to leave his community and get married if she was willing to do the same.

It is difficult to say what shocked Sister Patricia more—Philip's declaration or the degree to which she was blindsided by it. "I never saw it coming," she says. "I never felt anything. He was just a friend, like all my other friends. And when that sank in, I thought, 'Something's wrong here.' I recognized that I was very sexually out of touch."

What ensued was an all-out campaign on Sister Patricia's part to become what she calls a "whole woman." She went to counseling and did a lot of reading about psychology and sexuality, on the premise that if her own sexuality wasn't whole, then her spirituality couldn't possibly be either. "I really wanted to have my whole self working." Conveniently, Philip was similarly motivated. They took vacations together to romantic spots like Sister Patricia's uncle's cabin not far from where she grew up, having agreed that physical contact would be allowed if either was so inclined, as both craved a deeper understanding of themselves. Although the plan conflicted with the spirit of their vows, they justified it by saying that celibacy ought to be an informed choice. "We just wanted to be really alive," Sister Patricia says. "And he was, but I wasn't. I was never there sexually. I never wanted to do anything, and he never pushed me."

Soon after, Sister Patricia took a year off to be a full-time graduate student. Philip came to visit her on campus, and again nothing happened. After he left, Sister Patricia shared her frustration with a friend, lamenting how impossibly repressed she must be. Then the friend changed Sister Patricia's life when she casually offered, "Well, maybe you're gay." "All of a sudden—and I'm sure it's because I was out of that asexual milieu of religious life—I was able to say, 'Oh! Maybe I am!' "

Relatively safe in the liberal environment of a college campus, Sister Patricia took out lesbian literature from the library and rented movies about lesbian life. Astonishingly, she began to recognize herself. In one sense, it was a real homecoming. "But it was also absolutely horrifying"—given her impression of lesbians as "dykes and dorky people," she admits now. Even worse, a homosexual inclination seemed to undermine her identity as a religious. "My first thought was, 'I can't be a lesbian. I'm a nun. The church doesn't accept the actions of homosexual people' "—describing homosexual acts in an official document as "intrinsically disordered"—" 'and certainly not a homosexual nun. How could this be?' "

Given Sister Patricia's desire to understand her own sexuality, intimate relations with other nuns were inevitable. After the first time, she went to her superior and said, " 'This is what's happening, and I think I have to leave.' And the superior wisely said, 'Well, let's not move too quickly. Continue with the counseling, and don't make any rash decisions.' " So, like many others in the same anxious position, she tried to justify it. "We had been told to be celibate, because if you aren't, you're exclusive, and you can't be exclusive in religious life, and that sexuality takes you away from your ministry. All this stuff that I found out was a lie, because when I was in love, I was much more energetic, more giving to my ministry, much happier. Being in love is wonderful, right?"

But the rationale didn't hold up; ultimately Sister Patricia felt like a fraud, being both sexually active and a nun. "With a public vow of celibacy as most people understood it, it just wasn't right for me to believe one thing and profess another," she says. "My married sisters have to honor their vows. Besides, lesbians and gay men have been killed for being gay. And because I'm a nun"—living under the somewhat protective cloak of religious life, where same-sex roommates are common—"I can get away with it. It just doesn't seem fair."

Today Sister Patricia is somewhat at peace with herself, pointing out that "I'm still pretty sexually repressed. I don't often have sexual feelings. I clearly love being around women: I get energized by them and I give it back, and I don't give off the same kind of energy when I am with men. In fact, the more I realize who I am and the more I'm at home with it, the more I think, 'Well, if you weren't attracted to women, why would you be in this life?' " As Sister Patricia sees it, the typical woman religious is probably "more asexual or presexual than homosexual or heterosexual." In other words, many women have yet to recognize a basic and inevitable facet of their nature. "You look around and you see a lot of women really committed to ministry and sometimes in a sick way—they're real workaholics. Or they're depressed. Repressed sexuality comes out in all kinds of ways."

Still, nothing could be more depressing for a woman like Sister Patricia than the Catholic Church's disapproval of homosexuality. The church is so implacable on this score that in July of 1999 the Vatican ordered Sister Jeannine Gramick and her colleague Father Robert Nugent to discontinue their pastoral work with lesbians and gays. The Vatican had been investigating the ministry and concluded that the nun and the priest were, among other things, disseminating viewpoints that did not comply with the official Vatican position that homosexuality is a disorder and that homosexual acts are evil. "It's just devastating," says Sister

Patricia, who has been in counseling with Sister Jeannine. "It hits me at such a deep level that the church that I love and to which I have committed my life has such horrible thoughts and feelings about who I am at the core. Not that I believe any of it, but it just hurts." Which explains why Sister Patricia goes to Mass only sporadically—albeit without feeling for a moment that she is any less a sister.

For Sister Patricia and others like her, it is also frustrating that in some people's minds "lesbian" means "sexually active." Presumably such people can't imagine how knowing one's orientation could possibly matter if one truly intends to live a celibate life. Then again, it is still a new and jarring notion that nuns are just people, who might benefit from a degree of self-interest and self-regard.

MAD LOVE
Heeding the Call

❖

*D*ESPITE THE UTTERLY HUMAN
dilemmas that nuns struggle with every day, they are first and
last motivated by something otherworldly. What really separates
a nun from the rest of us is that deep and enduring sense of being
called to religious life. Today many religious are quick to say that
we are all called by God—be it to parenthood, teaching, public
service, or something else (presumably criminals are the luckless
souls who neither heard nor heeded their particular call). But
there seems to be a burning quality to the religious call that dis-
tinguishes it from all others. As disillusioned women are discov-
ering all the time, it is something larger and more complex than

simply wanting to do good in the world. "People come here saying, 'I want to help people,'" laments one religious-vocation director. "But that's not it. You can go help people right now! Being
called [to religious life] is about something else."

It is said that a woman doesn't choose this life, she is chosen.
A force from outside elicits an involuntary response. The obvious analog in lay life is the frothy feeling of falling in love. One
sister wells up as she describes a moment in church more than
thirty years ago when she was walking down the aisle and felt
her gaze and her body being pulled to the altar. She knew what
was happening, and she never doubted its significance. Dominican Sister Donna Quinn remembers being at the novitiate little
more than a month when all traces of ambivalence fell away. It
was Rosary Sunday. She was in chapel, and when she looked up,
her eyes locked on the crucifix looming above the head of the
novice mistress. "It was like I was levitating," she says. "I know
it sounds real hokey, but it was like a conversion inside of me.
And I never once had a question about whether I should stay."
During an especially difficult time in the novitiate, Franciscan
Sister Marge Eilerman began to doubt her fitness for the life.
Then one day while she was in the chapel, praying by a painted
pietà that she thought of as being her own special prayer space,
she heard God saying to her, "I have chosen you." "It was a mas-
culine voice," she remembers. "Very soft and very caring. I
remember feeling extremely peaceful." For some the call comes
as clearly and discernibly as a guiding hand laid along the small
of the back.

That romantic image is what most of us picture. So it is a surprise to learn that the call can also be a confusing and convoluted
business, requiring years of tortured introspection. Or that it fre-

quently springs from ordinary, earthly circumstances, like the desire to leave home, escape a boyfriend, or have an adventure. "At the time everyone was looking to get high," says one former cloistered nun. "I decided I was going to do the ecstatic thing with God. I knew it was either that or screw myself silly and have thirteen kids." But a real call gathers strength: While some women aren't catalyzed by the ethereal element, it is often what makes them stay.

Sisters in their seventies and eighties tend to describe the call as something that seized them in childhood and never let go. In conversation such women rarely reveal a hint of doubt or regret about the life they chose. Again the parallel to marriage pertains. The parents of middle-class baby boomers have tended to stay in their marriages no matter how flawed, as well as in the homes they bought forty years ago. Meanwhile, their children struggle, question, get divorced, and move every few years in their ongoing quest for self-fulfillment. Similarly, younger women's decision to enter religious life tends to be fraught in a uniquely modern way. Usually they describe a kind of ongoing tussle with God during those years before they entered, wherein they felt hounded by the idea of becoming a nun, as well as by God. For all of his majesty and elusiveness at other times, the Divine is often described as a very familiar and mildly annoying friend in these relentless back-and-forths. Many sisters recall their early conversations as jocular, chatty, and combative—something along the lines of "Okay, God, if You really want me You're going to have to show me." Or "Listen, God, I'm going to try this for a year. Just a year, that's it, that's all You get!" Befitting their modern outlook, they proceed cautiously—living with God for a while before taking the plunge into vows.

Today women aren't routinely shuttled from home to convent school to convent, remaining ignorant most of their lives to worldly temptations and alternatives. Thus their paths can be long and full of detours. Before becoming a Daughter of Charity, Sister Sara Stranz was sidetracked more severely than most.

From childhood she'd been imbued with the laudable ideal of Christian charity. "This is terrible," she says, "but we used to talk about pagan babies, 'pagan' of course referring to people who didn't believe in God. We'd take up collections to help the pagan babies over in Africa, and I remember being very touched by that." Her charitable instincts, along with seeing the movie *The Trouble with Angels* (1966)—sweet-natured fare about convent school—put the thought in Sara's mind that she'd one day like to become a sister.

But in her freshman year of high school, when the need to rebel and be in the hip group almost universally takes precedence over matters spiritual, Sara started taking drugs. The problem progressed steadily. Soon Sara was experimenting with serious substances like speed, cocaine, acid, and quaaludes. "I never shot up," she says. "But if you could snort it or swallow it, I'd do it." A low point came while she was attending a Jesse Colin Young concert. "I loved Jesse Colin Young, and I remember standing up and singing, clapping, and dancing. Then he walks off the stage. And I was like, 'What's he doing, man?' "—this in spot-on, drawn-out, druggie cadences that sound so strange coming from a sister. " 'He just came on the stage and he's going off!' And what had happened was, I'd blacked out and missed the whole concert." The problem escalated during Sara's junior year when her father, "the one person in my family who I felt really cared about me," was diagnosed with lung cancer. In time the disease was wasting him mercilessly. Unable to bear it, Sara helped herself to some of his painkillers.

She graduated with a 1.25 grade-point average and eventually took a job at an insurance company, doing drugs before work and during lunch. She was also going to church regularly, and somehow, through the narcotic haze, she could feel herself being pulled. Was it by God? It had to be. But to be absolutely sure, Sara threw all her drugs in the toilet and left town for a vocation retreat.

She was yelling at God the whole way there. "I want to know what's going on," she shouted out loud as she drove. "Are You going to have me become a sister and take away this tear I feel in my heart? I'm tired of feeling this pull, this struggle"—between the soothing escapism of drugs and the feeling that God had bigger plans for her. At the retreat Sara dropped to her knees and pleaded for God's help.

What followed was "one of those basic conversion experiences," as Sister Sara describes it. "I realized I had a problem and I could not stop it on my own—I was powerless. That is a very humbling experience. And in that moment I received the wonderful grace of God's forgiveness and strength. There was the sense that He was going to take care of it. Suddenly the desire to do drugs was gone." Even without the help of a detox program, Sara never did drugs again.

Intent on solidifying her relationship with God, who had after all just saved her life, Sara came to the Daughters of Charity. She was honest with them about her history with drugs. At their recommendation she received some counseling. And in 1983, at the age of twenty-five, Sara entered the community.

Now Sister Sara wears a simple blue knee-length habit, glasses, and a blue coiffe that resembles a kerchief. With her hair pulled back off her face, her eyes wide and bright, she looks scrubbed and renewed, smiling with a hint of evangelical fervor. She works in prisons and teaches religion while pursuing a master's degree in counseling. On most days she is awake and praying at 3:30 A.M., which leaves plenty of time for her *Jane Fonda Step Aerobics* tape before the day officially begins. All visible traces of the drug addict have disappeared.

In conversation the rhetoric of this former burnout runs toward the traditionally devout. She looks wounded at the thought of freshman girls having sex and laments the explicitness of rap-music lyrics. She thinks single-sex high schools are a good idea. And if a young girl does wind up pregnant, abortion—that time-honored "out" for so many a drug-taking concertgoer—is just not an option in Sister Sara's mind. Pregnancy, she says, "is an act of God. And I don't think we have the right to be playing God and take life away."

As for her onetime, decade-long dependence on drugs, is Sister Sara cured, or has she simply transferred her dependence? And if she *is* cured, was it really God's handiwork? Does it matter? It does to Sister Sara. Describing her instantaneous deliverance from a crippling vice, she says simply and confidently, "It was pure grace."

At the time of our conversation I was six months pregnant. Just before we parted, Sister Sara said a prayer for the baby. Then she made a small megaphone of her hands, leaned in toward my stomach, and happily shouted, "Can't wait for you to get here! It's a great world!"

* * *

Skeptics would have it that nuns are nuns because they are unmarriageable misfits who couldn't survive anywhere else. Without question there have been women over the years who entered the convent because they were looking for a safe haven. I have met several nuns, some as young as their early forties, who are seriously overweight. Given the secular world's notorious hostility toward women with weight problems, one can't help but wonder if such a factor plays a role, however subconscious, in the decision to retreat into a secluded community of women. On occasion it well may, but that is hardly typical. In the first place, the rigors of convent life test a woman's commitment several times a day. If she has come in search of security and safety, she will be grossly disillusioned upon undertaking the relentless trials of the novitiate.

Second, the abundance of unintentionally glamorous, well-adjusted nuns currently populating various orders suggests that most women have plenty of options before choosing to pursue this one. Such a person is the lean, blond Mary Lou Daoust, a Maryknoll sister and physician, who nearly lost her life several years ago in a head-on car collision in Guatemala, where she had spent seventeen years instructing native people in health care and disease prevention. Having broken the windshield with her head, Sister Mary Lou looked so bad that people were in the process of covering her with banana leaves on the side of the road where she'd been dragged from her car, as is the custom with the deceased in Guatemala.

Sister Mary Lou could have done anything with her life, but she didn't think the combination of service and spirituality that was practically guaranteed a Maryknoll missionary could be matched anywhere. Danger and excitement were part of the job.

Sister Mary Lou remembers hearing military tanks crunching along gravel roads. "Cars drove around with their lights out, and you just hoped they didn't stop in front of your house," she says in her relaxed way. Indeed, if Sister Mary Lou's experience is any indication, the idea of religious life as some sort of safe hideaway is patently absurd. In 1980, days before she was leaving for the mission in Guatemala, the two Maryknoll sisters (along with two other churchwomen) were murdered by the Salvadoran National Guardsmen. A few hours before Sister Mary Lou's send-off at the Maryknoll motherhouse, their bodies were found. Her sending ceremony was quickly replaced by a memorial Mass.

Some sisters, it seems, could have made the decision to enter in a vacuum, so pure and unwavering was their lifelong sense of being called. In most cases the sister's religious background— either her identification with the faith or her desire to compensate for its absence in childhood—plays a real role. Timing and serendipity are often factors, as they were with Pat Shutts, a forty-three-year-old postulant with the Greenville Poor Clares who grew up in a blue-collar industrial town south of Chicago.

"My dad worked in a steel mill, and my mom worked in a factory," she says, settling into a recliner in the monastery's guest quarters. She has short dark hair, glasses, and a pretty face that lights up as quickly and easily as it clouds with emotion. Her Midwestern laugh is spontaneous and hearty, until it is swallowed whole by what seems like a creeping melancholy. "My dad was an introvert, but when he expressed himself it was usually anger," Pat says, "especially with us women." By contrast, there was a soul-expanding joy in the Catholicism that she knew from visits to her great-grandmother's house. "There were pictures of the Sacred Heart on the wall, and when you walked in,

Great-Grandma would be praying the rosary. For me Catholicism was this warm, loving atmosphere that I felt in my great-grandmother's house." As early as third grade, Pat started to imagine that if she just sat quietly and concentrated hard enough, she could actually feel God.

Pat first thought about becoming a nun in junior high school; she loved reading the *Lives of the Saints* and used to sneak a book out of the library called *Bernie Becomes a Nun*, which told the story of a Maryknoll missionary. She was a typical kid in not wanting friends to know of her interest in such an earnest way of life. Yet she went through boyfriends, college, various jobs, and a short stay in another novitiate before seriously considering a cloistered existence. A visit with a Carmelite nun who was the friend of a friend changed Pat's mind forever about what at one time had seemed like a perverse misuse of a life.

"When my friend and I were on our way to see her, I remember thinking, 'What a waste,' " Pat says. " 'She doesn't do anything for God; she just prays all day behind these walls. It's stupid. She's probably this old pruney thing.' When we got there, they opened up a curtain, and she was behind a grille. And it was the first time I saw somebody's aura—like a light coming from a person. It made me shut my mouth." But Pat still wasn't ready to extricate herself from the secular rumpus she felt so comfortable in, with its endless promise of friends, drinks, and shopping excursions. Her job as the director of religious education at a big, prosperous parish didn't seem to conflict with any of that.

Then one day Pat was walking on the beach, waiting for the sun to come up. As she remembers it, "I was really impatient"—as much with herself as with the sun. She felt as though she should be doing something more than luxuriating in predictability and comfort. It is a common refrain among women who become nuns: She felt as though something was missing. "So I kind of cried out to God, and I remember feeling Him saying, 'The dawn will come. The time will come for you, too.'

"That was August. In September I had a dream that I was going to be a professed sister. I was putting on my habit for life and becoming a cloistered nun. The next day at work I saw a picture in the diocesan paper of these nuns in the habit that I was wearing in the dream. They were Poor Clares."

Nonetheless, it was the Carmelites she visited first. She spoke to a sister who remained behind a curtain. "It was just such a scary thing. I remember feeling the walls, getting weepy, saying I just want to be focused on God so much and I want to join. This poor nun listened to my story and finally said, 'You're too old, and I think from your story you should stay in active ministry. If you're really serious, go to the Poor Clares, because they'll take anyone.' " Pat laughs. "So I did." (That was an overstatement on the nun's part, although few orders are as strict and exacting as the Carmelites, in certain communities.)

And God's role in all this? To hear Pat tell it, God sometimes doubles as a guidance counselor. "He nudges you," she says. "It's as if He's saying, 'I think this might be good for you; look at this. But it's still your choice. You're free.' This is my weird little theology: I think of God as the ocean. You can look at how beautiful it is from the beach, or you can go swimming in it. I'd been coming in and out of the ocean," going on retreats and teaching religion, "but I think I had the desire to just be a fish."

Her evolution has not been easy. As a postulant, wearing her own skirts and cardigans in a sea of habits, she looks for the time being as if she is caught between worlds. At what point is such a person irretrievable? Can she be snatched back at the last minute, like those who have had a near-death experience? A secular person is tempted to ask the postulant, "Do you remember this life? Can you still recognize yourself in me?"

Pat hasn't yet been cleansed of her old life; she still misses doing "girl things" with her mother and buying presents for people (she has no money now and spends no time in stores). "Now I have to make things or find things," she says. "For Halloween I made little pumpkin projects for my nieces and nephews with stickers, and I made the stickers out of mailing labels—I colored them with pumpkin faces." She shrugs. "They liked them."

It can be terrible for the family, though. When they come to visit, Pat has to stay close by the monastery; she cannot go to a restaurant or to the movies with them. Early on she received an angry letter from her nephew, wondering why she would want to live like this and what it was exactly that she did all day. "So I wrote him a long letter back," Pat says, "with a moment-by-moment, blow-by-blow of what we do. And I told him I always think about him every day"—she starts to cry—"when I pray."

Whether or not Pat will make it to final vows and beyond is something even she doesn't know. Like most postulants, she has her worldly possessions stored at a relative's place, just in case.

Ambivalence plays a surprisingly significant role in many nuns' decision to enter religious life. For that reason most are disinclined to wax mystical. "It's called a 'call' because there is a sense that it is not coming from you," says Sister Anne Beth of the Little Sisters of Jesus. "It is something you feel outside yourself, and yet at the same time it speaks through who you are, your upbringing, your story. But we're all just people. I mean, we're just human beings." Only thirty-nine years old, she's been a nun for almost half her life. To have given herself over so totally for so long, surely she must have been summoned in a forceful way. But Sister Anne Beth refuses to romanticize. "You have your moments of doubt, like everyone does," she says flatly. "But like Peter said to the Lord, 'What else could I do?' Sometimes it's not more glamorous than that. I just think, 'But, Lord, what else would I do? What else could I do?' "

Other nuns seem to have been born with religious life in their bones; the only trial was in having to bide their time until they reached an age when entering the convent was an acceptable thing to do. And although their lives as nuns would be full of strange and painful surprises, a kind of thrumming constancy of commitment saw them through, contributing to that knowing, imperturbable air that is common among nuns who are "lifers."

A contemplative nature and fortuitous circumstances guided Sister Martha Ann Kirk along the path to the convent. While her decision to become an Incarnate Word sister had everything to do with the fact that relatives had attended the University of the Incarnate Word, her attraction to religious life dated back to childhood. As a girl she was drawn to prayer the way other kids were to kickball. "When I was eight years old, I remember saying at Mass one morning, 'Oh, God, guide me'—pretty heavy-duty for an eight-year-old," she says. As it happened, that very day a priest who was a vocation director for the diocese addressed her class, planting in their minds the idea that some of them might want to become priests and sisters when they grew up. Sister Martha Ann took it as a sign.

After all, she knew she wasn't cut out for the mainstream life of typical girls growing up in small Texas towns. "More and more I noticed that you had to wear the right clothes, you had to have the right eye makeup, and you had to go around with the right crowd," she says. "It made me so angry that football was absolutely the god in this town"—and cheerleading was a girl's highest calling. She shivers at the thought. Although she would never look at it this way, Sister Martha Ann got the last word. When it was proposed that the University of the Incarnate Word start a football team in the interest of attracting more applicants, some faculty members were strongly opposed. Sister Martha Ann was one of them, and the proposal was ultimately defeated.

All along, Sister Martha Ann knew she was destined for something else. "I kept feeling a kind of a gnawing call," she says, "and I knew I had to find out more about this." Which she did, in a clever way: She angled for the affections of a boy two years older, who had been to the seminary. She figured if they spent some serious time together, she could grill him about his experience.

"We did all the normal things you do," Sister Martha Ann says, "some kissing here and there and a lot of cruising around and talking and going to proms and movies. But I constantly asked him questions, like, 'What was the seminary like?' and 'How did you find out that you didn't belong there?' And he would talk to me about it. Then one night, after the prom, we were parking by the lake and I said, 'Now we're going to say the rosary together.' So there we were, saying the rosary, when the police came by and shined their spotlight on us, since you're not supposed to be parking there. Fortunately, all they did was tell us to move on. And I remember thinking, 'Maybe you are ready for the convent when you are in a car with your boyfriend late at night by a lake, saying the rosary.' "

*   *   *

On Easter weekend Sister Martha Ann drives along a roadside thick with pastel wildflowers to her mother's house in the small town of Cuero, Texas—the town, the house that Sister Martha Ann grew up in. Since her father died in 1971, she and her mother have grown even closer; in its intensity and slightly Southern Gothic flavor, their relationship resembles the mythic mother-daughter bond at the center of Larry McMurtry's *Terms of Endearment*.

"Marth'!" Ada calls out, arms, eyes, and smile wide as Sister Martha Ann drives up.

They go into town, which is still recovering from the Guadalupe River's overflowing several months before and leaving a third of the residents homeless. In addition, a number of small businesses are closed or closing, thanks to a Wal-Mart that has moved in nearby. Sister Martha Ann and Ada take in a couple of exhibits at some local museums: a thorough display of the undeniably spectacular Texas wildflowers, as well as a salute to the cowboy called "Cattle and Cowhands." The latter features Ada's own saddle, as well as family photographs; Sister Martha Ann hails from a prominent Cuero family that has been working a six-hundred-acre ranch since the 1870s. Back in the car, as they meander home, Sister Martha Ann and Ada chatter happily; Sister Martha Ann seems incapable of the impatience that rises in any other daughter who is spending time with her talkative mother.

At home Ada displays a number of family photos on a folding screen that tell the story of Sister Martha Ann's life. The early ones, with their yellowed patina of fifties family fun, could be from any middle-American home. There is one of an infant Martha Sue riding a float as the winner of the Miss Baby Beauty contest, another of her as a toddler sitting in an inner tube wearing red nail polish, and many of Martha Sue hamming it up in theatrical costumes or assuming dance positions. About midway down the screen there is a striking photograph of a family get-together at the center of which is Martha Sue with tousled blond hair, wearing a sexy, shoulderless dress, looking for all the world like Marilyn Monroe. It is startling to learn that only days later she entered the convent; her hair had just been bobbed for that purpose. Similarly, on a wall in Ada's study, there is a large framed photograph of Martha Sue that same year, all shoulders and curves and shapely thighs in a dark tutu, fishnet stockings, and a tiara. In all of these pictures Martha Sue wears a placid smile that makes her look as if she's got a secret.

Suddenly this gentle, creative spirit is pictured everywhere in funereal black. Perhaps the most shocking photograph from this era is one of Martha Sue, now Sister Martha Ann, entertaining her family at the Incarnate Word motherhouse. Her energetically smiling parents and brother are arrayed around this column of darkness—Sister Martha Ann's impish face encased in headgear, the girl in chiffon skirts and tutus devoured whole by the habit. Comic relief comes a little way down, with a photograph of Ada vamping in a shin-length habit. Vatican II was under way, and the order was experimenting with different styles and skirt lengths. Having helped out with the sewing, Ada was modeling her latest creation.

It was so hard on Ada, losing Martha Sue like that. Before Vatican II giving up a daughter to the convent felt a little bit like a death in the family. But a real call is hard to fight. Ada wrote an article about it for the Alamo *Messenger*, in which she recalled her reaction to the news that Martha Sue wanted to enter the convent right away.

"Marth', what will we do without you?" she writes. "Every

minute of every day of your life you have been the light and joy in this house. After sixteen short years, you would take this light and joy out of our lives?"

And the inevitable answer comes:

"I love you, Daddy, and Rob so much, but I think I love God more. I've never really asked you and Daddy for anything—you've always given me everything *before* I could ask—but, I'm asking for your blessing and permission now."

They gave it, of course. What else could they do? And they never knew their daughter in quite the same way again.

On Easter Sunday, Sister Martha Ann and Ada drive out to Martha's brother Robbi's place, a rambling farmhouse that used to belong to their grandfather. The long, narrow, pitted road leading to it runs past a feral pig trap and a one-room schoolhouse that Ada used to ride her horse to when she was a teacher there. Hawks glide on fringed wings above the large oak out front. It was a family ritual every Easter to pull Spanish moss from the tree, make it into a nest, and decorate it with wildflowers such as Indian blankets, primroses, and buttercups in hopes that the Easter bunny would come by and deposit a few eggs inside.

But Robbi's two lovely and fast-growing daughters are a little old for that now; like many a Texan teenage girl, they are preoccupied with school, boys, clothes, and sports. The older one drives Sister Martha Ann and Ada several hundred yards down the dirt road, eager to show off her new skills behind the wheel.

Robbi's wife, Cindy, who is blond and lithe in her shorts and sneakers, puts out a meal of barbecued chicken, brisket, corn, potatoes, and baked beans. Sister Martha Ann, wearing a peasant blouse that she made herself, samples some of the nonmeat items. Vegetarianism seems scandalously out of place here, as does a disdain for cheerleading (both Ada and Cindy used to be cheerleaders, and soon one of the nieces will be one, too). It is a clear measure of the strength of Sister Martha Ann's call that she could so wholeheartedly reject such an ingrained model of what a Texas girl should be.

The fact of the call is in some ways less dramatic than the decision whether or not to heed it. Even in secular life the remarkable person is the one with an ability to recognize an opportunity when it comes along and then act on it. In religious life that means turning your back on everything you once held dear. Still, there are many nuns who claim there was no decision, no act of will involved. They had simply been hounded by the prospect from a young age; as a result, they didn't so much muster the courage to take a chance as they finally surrendered to the relentless goading.

Like love, the quality of the call can change over time. It can lose its immediacy and its power and fade the way a romance does. For some women the pull of the vocation slackens to the point where leaving religious life feels natural, if not exactly easy. At least partly to stave off such gloomy developments, most orders encourage sisters to go on regular retreats, during which they can reexamine and renew their commitment.

For being called to religious life is a rare and mysterious thing. And being called twice is something extraordinary indeed.

During her novitiate with the Franciscan Sisters of Allegany, Nancy Shively, who is now a Poor Clare, seemed an unlikely candidate for religious life. "I was always asking questions, and I was always in trouble," she says with a laugh. In 1968 the order started modifying its habits, beginning with those worn by the professed sisters. Nancy was only a novice at the time, but she had seen it written on a blackboard that habits could be shortened to three inches below the knee. She got so excited, she and a friend ran down to the sewing room, cut their habits shorter, and hemmed them up in time for evening prayer. Shortly thereafter Sister Nancy was summoned by the novice directress, who sternly rebuked her for being a bad influence. This was nothing new.

Her taste for mischief notwithstanding, something serious and abiding had propelled her here. She first felt it during college at St. Bonaventure in southwestern New York. "I was at a keg party chugging some beers and smoking some cigarettes, and suddenly I felt very empty. 'This isn't it,' I thought. 'There's something big missing.' And I left the party almost as soon as I arrived. When I got back to the dorm, I was hysterical. I ran up the stairs and hid behind the washing machine, because I didn't want anyone to find me, and I cried my eyes out. I just knew that I was supposed to do something other than this. That was the moment." But if Nancy was looking for meaning in her life, couldn't she just as easily have joined the Peace Corps? She says no. "I knew God was putting a finger on me, calling me to a deeper relationship. It felt like a personal invitation."

Serendipity influenced the course of events. When she was a senior in high school, Nancy had mentioned to her father that she might like to go to the convent someday. "He thought, 'Where have I failed as a father that my daughter would want to run away to the convent?' " Sister Nancy says. So he made a deal with her: She could do what she wanted, just as long as she gave college a try first. So in 1964 she went to St. Bonaventure, which had been her father's first choice for her. The school had far more men than women attending, having been an all-male school just a decade before; clearly he thought she might find a future husband there. What he didn't consider was the fact that the Allegany Franciscan motherhouse was right down the street. The nuns were in charge of the girls' dormitory, a former motherhouse itself, which served as temporary lodging while a proper dorm was being built. So the night Nancy rushed back to the dorm, she practically ran into the arms of the Allegany sisters who minded the front desk. Noting her distress, they went looking and found Nancy behind the washing machine. They spoke to her encouragingly of these early intimations of a call.

The following year the new dorm opened. If Nancy had entered college any later than she did, she probably would never have met the sisters.

Once she'd taken her final vows, Sister Nancy went on to an accomplished career that culminated in the high-pressure world of hospital administration. She wore business suits, relaxed with a beer and pizza at the end of a hard day, and accumulated thousands of frequent-flier miles. She was a model of the well-adjusted post–Vatican II sister, at home in the world. Sister Nancy was an extraordinarily active Allegany Franciscan for twenty-eight years.

Then, in 1993, serendipity—or was it fate?—struck again. As it happened, 1993 was the eight-hundredth anniversary of the death of Clare, foundress of the Poor Clare nuns, who are spiritually allied with the Franciscans. One day, while they were living in Florida, Sister Nancy and her roommate, Annie, received an invitation from the Greenville Poor Clares asking Franciscans to mark the anniversary of the death of Clare by coming for a visit to their monastery. "This was totally unheard of," says Sister

Nancy, "because Poor Clares have always been cloistered. No one was ever allowed inside." Sister Nancy had no interest in cloistered life. But Annie convinced her they should go.

"We came the last week of June," Sister Nancy says. "And I wasn't here twenty-four hours before I was in the choir, and . . . All I can tell you is I had a very real experience of God saying to me three things. First of all, 'Welcome home.' Second of all, 'You've found what you've always been looking for, and you didn't even know you were looking for it.' And thirdly, 'This is really what you entered religious life for in the first place.' It was so clear, so shocking, so present to me the whole week I was here. I walked around in a daze: Something was happening, something deep and pregnant. I didn't know what it was, but I was scared to death. I wanted to run away from it, but I also wanted to run to it at the same time.

"The end of the week came, and Annie and I both cried our eyes out as we said good-bye, because it had been such a powerful experience. We were driving home in silence, we were so overcome. I was thinking, 'Something happened back there and I don't know what, but I know I have to figure it out. It couldn't possibly be vocational, because I don't have a vocation problem. I'm not having a midlife crisis.' And suddenly Annie said, 'Nancy, I'm so glad we did this, because now I know for sure that cloistered life isn't for me.'

"And I said, 'Annie, I'm not so sure.' "

Sister Nancy wrote to the community, and a few months later she returned for an extended stay, during which she and God wrestled. She'd given everything she had for twenty-eight years to the Allegany congregation; asking her to give up all that seemed unconscionable. "They're my life, my other self. You can't ask me to walk away from that," Sister Nancy told God. In addition, she'd grown accustomed to the jazzy, almost yuppie life of a high achiever, sometimes flying to three cities a week for meetings. What would such a woman do with herself in a monastery? But God is full of surprises. Sometimes His choices aren't the obvious ones. "I remember the day clearly: It was December sixth, and I was out in the hermitage writing in my journal, and suddenly I just burst out crying hysterically, and I heard myself saying, 'I know, God. I know. I know. This is it. I know that it's really You. This is Your call.' I couldn't fight it anymore."

Three months later Sister Nancy entered the Poor Clare community. That was six years ago.

When a secular person first meets someone as vivacious and capable as Sister Nancy, it is tempting to indulge a superficial reaction: Nancy, don't lock yourself away—we need you out here. But then there is the Nancy who steps softly, circumspectly, into the chapel on a hushed spring morning. She assumes her place in the choir. As she opens her breviary and reads a psalm, her voice rising and blending with those of her sisters all around her, she looks as if she is in an altered state. A quite visible peacefulness smooths her skin and lights her face. At such a time it is difficult to doubt that Sister Nancy has found her way home.

There are limitless varieties of love, although sometimes it seems as if there are only two: the toe-tingling kind that one falls into and the meandering kind that reveals itself over time. The question of which is better is the unanswerable stuff of sonnets and songs.

It is similar with the call. To say the least, having a mystical vision seems a rousing validation of one's spiritual potential. But the call that gradually accumulates power, going from inkling to inevitability, is uniquely persuasive. The woman who honors her vows after admitting doubt and facing difficulties reaps the very human reward of having struggled and won.

Sister Diana feels a strange mix of solemnity and giddiness as she looks at the new habit hanging on the curtain rod at the door of her cell. Her black cappa, the cape for special occasions, hangs there as well. This is her new uniform, her garb for all time. Tomorrow she will make her solemn profession—that is, she will close the door on this life forever and enter the state of grace for which her whole life has seemed inexorable preparation.

In a way these five years of formation have gone quickly. It seems a short time ago that Diana was a dutiful employee at a publishing company in Manhattan, watching her friends' jaws drop as she told them of her plans to enter a monastery. But there were hints for anyone who was paying attention. For instance, the order had supplied her with a long list of things to bring, which necessitated lunchtime shopping sprees yielding things like a dozen tubes of toothpaste and a sewing kit. There was a surreal quality to this period of preparation. When Diana went to buy two pairs of plain black shoes, the puzzled salesman had to ask why. Diana hesitated and then, in very un-nunlike fashion, lied, telling the man that she'd be helping out in her sister's catering business, and the shoes were just part of the uniform. The salesman didn't seem especially convinced. He threw in a few tins of black shoe polish for free. Then there was the issue of sleepwear. Unaware that printed fabric is acceptable at the monastery, Diana searched the stores for an all-white nightgown. Finally she found and ordered the perfect one—from Victoria's Secret.

Since Diana was still living at home with her parents, there was little in the way of possessions to disperse. Her parents picked up the lease on her Toyota. Diana's mother and sister took her clothes, earrings, and perfume, and the first few times they showed up at the monastery wearing her favorite scarf or a beloved scent were hard to take. The only item of real value was Diana's brass bed, which remained where it was. She also had a large library of spiritual reading, which the novice mistress had said she could bring, despite the usual limit of three books per entrant. A co-worker bought most of her CDs. Diana gave her Edith Piaf collection to another colleague, who shared her love of the brooding chanteuse. Delighted by the CDs, the co-worker promised to keep them for Diana, who had to explain gently that they were hers to keep.

Even with its heavy air of finality, this period of shedding skin was exhilarating. Diana felt free and playful, like someone who had just quit a dreary job. One day, while walking to the subway after a farewell lunch with a friend, Diana was talking about what she'd be leaving behind. Suddenly she stopped, looked up at the tall buildings, and said melodramatically, "Good-bye, New York!"

A man roughly Diana's age materialized by her side. "I'm sorry, but I couldn't help overhearing your conversation," he said. "Where are you going anyway? It sounds like another planet!"

The two women broke out laughing. "Close enough," Diana said, leaving the thoroughly confused eavesdropper to ponder that.

A few weeks later, on a sunny day in November, a van pulled up to the curb in front of Diana's house. A nun from the monastery, along with their unofficial caretaker and their pet German shepherd, had come for Diana. With her father at work and her mother baby-sitting at her sister's, Diana was in the house all alone. The caretaker loaded Diana's suitcases and boxes into the back of the van while she tried to say good-bye to her cat, who'd scooted under the bed. Then she moved toward the door without looking back, having promised herself that she wouldn't. As they pulled away from the house, Diana's eyes—pointed straight ahead—welled up.

Thirty minutes later she was in the bathroom off the parlor at the monastery, changing out of her skirt and blouse into the postulant's polyester blue jumper. Some guests and friends, including her college crush, Tom, were seated in the chapel, having come to witness Diana's entrance ceremony. Diana knelt in the first pew, eyeing the sanctuary door, notable for the fact that it has no doorknob. Finally the door opened, and the prioress's head peeked out. As instructed, Diana walked up to the sanctuary, entered the enclosure, and stepped over the threshold into her new life. The other sisters were processing into the choir behind the hugely symbolic grille, singing Psalm 122: "I rejoiced when I heard them say: 'Let us go to God's house . . . ' "

Diana and the prioress entered the choir last. Now Diana was behind the grille, too—a quietly, profoundly shocking sight for her friends in the pews.

There were readings from Scripture and a closing prayer from the prioress:

> *Lord, You have given your servant, Diana*
> *the desire to serve You.*
> *Complete the work You have begun.*
> *Make her gift of self wholehearted*
> *and bring this first beginning*
> *to its perfect end. . . .*

With hugs and kisses the sisters officially welcomed Diana into the community. Then she went to the parlor to spend a few more minutes with her guests, only now she had to see them from behind a wooden counter—a long, waist-height barricade. This was her life now. Only for reasons of real necessity, such as doctor appointments, would she ever find herself on the other side of it again.

Surprisingly, the radical break from secular life isn't the hardest part of being here. Neither is the grueling schedule, which often starts at 2:45 A.M., when Diana rises for what she calls rosary guard. Her community observes perpetual adoration of the Eucharist and perpetual rosary, which means that around the clock sisters take turns sitting before the Blessed Sacrament and saying the rosary, which comprises the Joyful Mysteries, the Sorrowful Mysteries and the Glorious Mysteries of Christ's life, death, and resurrection. The person praying ponders each scene of each mystery while moving her fingers along the rosary beads, thereby entering ever deeper into a state of prayer and identification with the life and suffering of the Lord. It is hoped that the prescribed, almost mathematical nature of the exercise will facilitate the rush of heart and soul into an expansive, prayerful place, much as a grounding three-four rhythm enables limitless flights of fancy in song and dance. Perpetual adoration and perpetual rosary ensure that there is someone with Christ, praying to Him, at all times.

In preparation for rosary guard, Sister Diana wears the night habit to bed—a lighter-weight version of what she wears during the day. So when she awakens, she need only jump up, fasten her leather belt with fifteen-decade rosary attached, fling on her scapular, and position her veil on her head. She is dressed in about a minute and a half. Staying awake can be a challenge, but Sister Diana takes solace in St. Thérèse of Lisieux's once saying, "The Lord loves me just as much when I am asleep as He does when I am awake." And if she's lucky, Sister Diana will catch another hour of sleep after rosary guard, which she will need for the day ahead, with its chores and jobs like mopping hallways and processing library books between regular visits to the chapel. By 10 P.M. Sister Diana is in bed, bone-tired.

She has no trouble with hard work and prayer. It's the little things that tend to rankle. She knows it sounds petty, but she misses her special shampoos and soaps—in here it's Irish Spring, and Sister Diana doesn't like Irish Spring. The nuns do break with pre–Vatican II tradition in shaving their legs and underarms, though, which was a great relief to her. They also use hand lotion, a blessed necessity after submerging their arms in hot water for long periods during laundry duty. Sister Diana also has to get used to the abject abuse of tresses and locks that is the norm in monasteries. In lay life Diana spent a fair amount of time and money on fashionable hairstyles. Now she gives herself hasty, haphazard haircuts. If she has to leave the monastery for any reason, she figures she would have to wear a wig.

But by far the greatest challenge is living in community. Breaking out of the self-serving, individualistic mind-set that prevails in the secular world has been a ceaseless challenge. Add to that the frank and direct mode of communication she was reared on, and Sister Diana has had a lot of adjusting to do. Up to now she'd always thought she was an easygoing person. In fact, she is realizing, she can be impatient and bossy. Almost weekly the novice mistress advises her to tone it down, and Sister Diana is repulsed by the whiff of rebuke. But in the vacuumlike environment of the monastery, hurt feelings and misunderstanding can be poisonous. There is no escaping—no driving around the block or having a few drinks at a bar to blow off steam. Sometimes it is so difficult to observe the cornerstone idea that the women have all come together to live harmoniously, united in their thorough-going focus on God.

Sister Diana tries to heed the compline reading that advises against letting the sun go down on your wrath. But it's hard. She felt something akin to wrath just the other day, when chores beckoned while she was studying. They could wait, couldn't they? Well, no, the novice mistress told her. Sister Diana has yet to absorb the nettlesome monastic principle that requires a capacity for peaceful acceptance, even of the seemingly silliest rules and customs. In a monastery, being serenely amenable is valued more highly than being right—calling to mind the scene from *The Nun's Story* where the superior suggests to a willful, prideful novice that she prove her humility by intentionally flunking an exam. Sister Diana has to sublimate her desires to the good of the community, which often means keeping her smart ideas to herself. Grudgingly, she is coming to realize that the vow of obedience is easy when you are doing things you want to do. As an opinionated woman in her early thirties surrounded by aged veterans of self-sacrifice, she still has a way to go.

On the positive side, there have been some beautiful and sustaining moments in community. Once, when Sister Diana was smarting from yet another admonition from the novice mistress, an older sister came over and said, "Keep your head up, kid. I'm praying for you." That was priceless. So are the occasional laughs. Sister Diana has a funny exchange going with one sister: Whenever they pass each other in the halls, they discreetly and silently hold up a hand and split their fingers, exchanging the Vulcan greeting from *Star Trek*. Sister Diana giggles just thinking about it.

In no way do the difficulties outweigh the rewards, which is why Sister Diana views her solemn profession as she does: Tomorrow is the most important day of her life. At the suggestion of the prioress she remains "in retreat" today, staying collected and contemplative, gathering strength for the momentous passage, which means praying the rosary during recreation while the chatter and laughter of her sisters filter through the wall. Then Sister Diana joins them in the chapter hall and indulges in an old tradition, a special chapter of faults for sisters about to be professed. She walks to the middle of the chapter hall and kneels. Then she extends her arms in cruciform and says, "Dear sisters, I humbly beg your pardon for the many failings in charity I have committed since my entrance," before enumerating some minor transgressions. Then she lies down on the floor on her right side, her head resting under her arm, performing a once common public penance. After a few seconds the prioress asks Sister Diana to rise, at which point she goes around the room giving the "pax"—a big hug of peace—to each sister. Tears are running down the prioress's face as Sister Diana approaches. In an exquisite gesture of charity, she asks for Sister Diana's pardon for her own failings as well.

That night Sister Diana repairs to her cell, a six-by-nine warren with walls of faux oak and stucco, a transom window over the doorway, and a white curtain for a door. Inside are a narrow bed, a small wooden bookshelf, a desk, a lamp, an alarm clock, a water tumbler, an ornate wall crucifix, a holy-water font by the doorway, and a glow-in-the-dark rosary. On this night there are also several gifts: more rosaries, holy cards, stationery, and candles on Sister Diana's bed and desk. They are from her sisters, of course. According to tradition, they have decorated the "bridal chamber." Sister Diana wells up at their thoughtfulness. Then she crawls into bed and sleeps by candle-light.

The next morning she is refreshed but a little annoyed to see a thick fog engulfing the monastery. "Come on, dear Lord," she thinks, "it is, after all, my wedding day. I've got to have beautiful weather!" (Later on, God actually complies.) Then Sister Diana fulfills another preparatory obligation, writing down the names of everyone who has been significant to her on her journey here. She also writes down all the names of people who have asked to be remembered at her profession. She fills three sheets of paper, rolls them up, and tucks them in her bra. Not that the names will be recited or read; it's just that she wants them close to her heart.

Sister Diana pulls on her new habit and starts downstairs at 9:15 A.M., her cappa swirling around her as she walks through the hallways along the polished oak floors to the sacristy. As she stops at the entrance alcove to the chaplain's quarters and waits for the prioress and novice mistress, she can see two of the broth-ers from the order fussing with candles. They are so preoccupied with this task, they don't even hear Sister Diana when she whis-pers, "Hi, guys!" The priests are more relaxed; there are hugs and chatter, until the chaplain reminds everyone of the important business at hand. "It's getting late," he says. "We'd better get going."

Sister Diana takes her place in line behind the brothers, adjust-ing the hoods on their capes, making everything look perfect, like a bride fussing with her bridesmaids' taffeta bows. The brothers seem unnerved by this. Only Sister Diana is relaxed, so sure is she that she has made the right decision.

Then the organist strikes a key, their cue to begin processing up the aisle. A brother bearing a six-foot brass cross is the first. Others follow with candles. Sister Diana is behind them, her smile forcing its way across her face as she nods to the guests on either side of the aisle: There is her mother, brother and sister, her nephews, friends from college, including Tom with his wife and small daughter. Once the procession arrives at the sanctuary, Sister Diana catches Tom's eye and smiles.

Father Jim offers opening remarks: "Well, Diana, the presence of so many of your brothers in the order today should leave no doubt in your mind about the high esteem and love we have for you—and for all the nuns and your role in the order." Then she settles in for great, solemn stretches of liturgy. She is aware of her friends and family in the pews, but as the spirit of the ceremony overtakes her, the faces grow fuzzy and recede. They represent another life, the one behind her, after all.

Then it comes time for the day's heart-stopping moment, the prostration, during the Litany of the Saints. Sister Diana goes to the middle of the sanctuary in front of the steps leading to the altar. Then she sinks to her knees on the ornate carpet and stretches out facedown and lies there for several minutes like a dead moth. It is a gesture of death—of throwing herself at Christ's feet and giving up her life for Him. Holding her body in the form of a cross, she makes the ultimate sacrifice: *I am nailing myself to the cross as You did and dying to this world.*

While she is lying on the floor, Sister Diana is neither distressed nor transported. Rather, she is concentrating on her breathing. Her head rests on her chin, as her eyeglasses make it impossible for her to lay her face sideways. She remains in this position during the Litany of the Saints, wherein the community asks each of the saints to "pray for us."

After the last saint has been implored, Sister Diana pulls herself up, ascends the stairs, and kneels before the prioress, who is sitting in a chair by the altar. This is the high point, the moment of her profession. The order's *Book of Constitutions* is lying in the prioress's hands. Then Sister Diana slides her own hands, palms up, beneath the prioress's and the book she holds. Which is to say, she is at once embracing the community and putting her life in its hands. The two women have grown close over the years; Sister Diana wrote letters to the prioress for more than a decade before even entering the monastery, seeking insight and guidance as she traveled the winding way of a potential vocation. And now it has come to this: a compressed and shimmering moment of truth. Sister Diana begins her profession formula, promising obedience to God, to blessed Mary, to the founder of the order, as well as to the prioress. She looks up as she says this, but the prioress does not. Perhaps the moment is just too intense. Sister Diana is steady as an orator, until the final line: "I will be obedient to you, and to your successors until death."

She signs the document of profession on the altar. Then she kneels in front of it as the nuns sing, from behind the wooden lattice screen that recently replaced the metal grille they had used for many years, "*Amo Christum*"— "I love Christ into whose bridal chamber I shall enter. . . ." Father Jim stands before Sister Diana and begins the long, lyrical Prayer of Solemn Consecration: "Father in heaven, the desire to serve You is Your gift. . . ." Sister Diana closes her eyes and lets the words sink in. The tedium of time falls away—she feels both weak and strong. "Send the fire of the Holy Spirit to warm into flame the resolve He has kindled in the heart of Your daughter," Father Jim says. And at that moment the Lord seems to say to Sister Diana, "Okay, Diana?" She nods.

At the end of the prayer Father Jim places his hand on Sister Diana's head and blesses her veil. Then he sprinkles her ring with holy water, thoroughly soaking the case. When he lifts out the ring, it is dripping, and Sister Diana has to laugh.

She holds out her hand. "Which finger?" Father Jim whispers sharply. She wiggles the fourth one on her right hand. He slips it on. The ring used to be worn by another sister who has since died, and when Sister Diana passes, the ring will be given to someone else. From this moment on, she owns nothing. However, the nuns can temporarily personalize their rings with an inscription of their choosing. For her ring Sister Diana selected *Consummatum est*—"It is finished." Christ's last words on the cross.

A SEPARATE PEACE

The Future of the American Nun

❖

*I*T HAS BEEN THREE MONTHS SINCE Sister Diana made her solemn profession. On a frigid day under a steel-colored sky, I walk up to the monastery and search for an entrance. There are a couple of doors without handles or knobs; it feels as if the place is sealed shut. The rumbling thickness of the Gothic monastery's history is almost palpable—no one would hear if I knocked or shouted. As I walk around the building, I sense that I am being watched.

Finally I find a door with a bell at the back of the building. When I press I am buzzed in to a dark vestibule. There is an old monastic turn behind me; it looks like a barrel with a bullet hole in its side. For centuries, turns have enabled cloistered nuns to receive people and packages without exposing themselves to the outside world. A small, shy-sounding, disembodied voice welcomes me from the general direction of the turn. When I say I have an appointment with Sister Diana, the voice sends me around to the front of the building to a parlor located just off the chapel, which is lined in stained glass of crimson, royal blue, amber, olive, and gold.

The room is silent. There is a crucifix on the wall and a photograph of some elated nuns meeting Pope John Paul II. A few chairs face the wooden barricade that is, for the moment, completely shuttered.

Suddenly a shutter comes down—Sister Diana unlatching and hoisting. At a broad-shouldered five foot nine in her long white habit and black veil, she is smiling and efficient, placing a tray before me. On it are a thermos full of coffee, sugar, butter, a creamer, and a two-inch-thick wedge of bread laced with raisins and pecans. Sister Diana's round eyes are green, and her eyeglasses are gold-rimmed, their fine gold earpieces tucked in under the veil. She is wearing a wristwatch, as well as the ring she received on her profession. Free of makeup, her face has that bright, scrubbed look so common among younger nuns.

We talk of the lousy weather; she tells me about the flu epidemic that just ripped through the monastery. Sister Diana is a fast and animated talker; her sisters describe her as being kind of "wired." Sometimes her deceptively soft tone gets a little insistent, suggestive of someone less intent on being understood than heard. When she giggles and gestures with her hands, her rosary clicking as she shifts around in her chair, a familiar layperson seems to be peeking out and waving from somewhere behind the habit.

Despite her girlish energy, Sister Diana has some of the mythic serenity one associates with nuns. She seems to have taken a soulful possession of this place; she is proud to be here. Not that the challenges aren't regular and intense. She still misses her favorite perfumes and shampoos, although on the bright side, "We don't have bad-hair days," she says. "Bad-veil days, maybe."

Although the life is undeniably difficult, Sister Diana is convinced that God is with her always, and if she is too distracted to notice, He will find ways to make His presence known. The other day, while she was taking a bath and feeling weepy for one reason or another, a roll of toilet paper plopped into the tub. Sister Diana had to laugh, never doubting that this was some sort of sign. "Okay, Lord, I know," she said to herself. "Time to lighten up."

It is a fit, this life, as Sister Diana says. She always knew that it would be. At several points during her formation, she was required to meet with the monastery's council, a panel of nuns, and report on her spiritual progress. In one such session the council asked her, "Do you feel a strong interior commitment to this life?"

"I'll put it to you this way," Sister Diana remembers saying. "There are times when I say to myself, 'Were you ever not a nun?' "

Sister Diana shows me a photograph of herself on a college trip in Paris. She is unrecognizable in her loud and fashionable purple coat, accented by a decorative scarf. In the picture Diana's eyes are dark with makeup, and her naturally straight hair is full of curls. "I had a body wave or whatever they call it," she says. The purple coat was her favorite. The prioress allowed her to bring it to the monastery. "When I wear it, the sisters say they can see me from quite a distance." She laughs.

I wonder if she and that woman on the Left Bank are the same person. According to Sister Diana, in many ways they still are. For instance, when she was joking around with her college friends at the reception following her solemn profession, it was just like old times. There was nothing different about the way they treated each other. Sister Diana looks at the photograph for a few more seconds. "But yeah, sometimes I say, 'Gosh, where is she now?' "

The bell starts to clang, calling the sisters to choir. In midsentence Sister Diana rises and pulls in the food tray. There is no hesitating when the Lord calls. Quickly she says good-bye as she hauls a shutter into place, walling herself in. And suddenly the room that had been echoing with chatter only seconds ago is silent, but for a muffled "Bless you" from behind the wall.

It is breathtaking, seeing a woman of thirty-three in this life. The spirited fidelity that Sister Diana radiates seems like a sign of hope for the institution. But her kind is dangerously rare.

Most women who have been called to Christ are motivated by a burning inevitability. Yet those who leave religious life can be every bit as ardent. For many, what began as the openhearted heeding of a call turned into a mechanical exercise—a dutiful observance of an archaic practice. The inherent rigidity of religious life no longer made sense in a society that was increasingly driven by personal freedom. Such women realized that they could still be Christian and charitable without submitting to the self-denying strictures of the convent. "Sisters don't really live in community anymore. What's so different about them and their commitment and me and my commitment?" says a former Franciscan. "If living the gospel life is really what Christianity is about, I can do that as a married woman. I just didn't see it as a viable life, and I did not want to find myself fifty years old and saying, 'Oh, my goodness, there's nothing here.' " For one former nun who left after two decades of selfless service, summoning the courage to go was like outfoxing death. She improvises a psalm: "My life like a bird has escaped the snare of the fowler."

Many who have left were eager, finally, to escape an institution that seemed to have grown moribund. Communities are forced into taking increasingly desperate measures to sustain them- selves, one of the cheekier being something called Adopt-a-Nun, dreamed up by some New Jersey nuns who each offer personal prayers for a donation of a hundred dollars. One sixty-seven- year-old former priest solicited pledges for his 3,200-mile bike ride, the proceeds of which go to helping aging religious. A Bene- dictine community in Indiana has resorted to aggressive and highly secular marketing techniques to pinpoint and recruit potential postulants. According to *The Wall Street Journal*, the nuns have consulted with high-powered strategists, like the cre- ative director from an ad agency who advised, "We are like an ice-cream shop. We have to lure the customer to knock on the door and try out our flavors."

Subscribe to a Catholic newspaper or magazine and suddenly your mailbox will be flooded with little mass-produced medals, crosses, and prayer cards in the hope that you'll send some money in exchange. Then there are the ceaseless unvarnished requests for charitable contributions, like the plea from a Dominican community that goes, "Who was your most memo- rable Sister? Perhaps it was the Sister who prepared you for your First Holy Communion, or the Sister who quizzed the class end- lessly to prepare you for Confirmation. You remember her name and probably the class but mostly the very special way she touched you and changed your life forever. You will never forget her! And, I can assure you . . . she has never forgotten you, either." Then comes the request for money to help these ill and aged women. There is no pretense here about their mission and the money it requires. These women are desperate, plain and simple, and they need your help. What a strange state of affairs for people cast for so long in the role of perpetual giver.

The plight of the institution grows starkly apparent when one considers how many large, dormlike novitiates are now being turned into nursing homes for ailing nuns; the places feel eerily futuristic, echoing with the clang of walkers and the whir of automated conveyances. During Mass at the Loretto mother-house, the inner wall of the chapel is lined with wheelchairs holding frail, slumped sisters. Queuing up for Communion is out of the question; instead the priest brings the host directly to them. Every effort has been made to ease the sisters' physical burdens, which they appreciate. Sitting snug in a kind of motor-ized La-Z-Boy, one sister patted the chair and said, "Whoever invented this thing should be canonized."

Since Vatican II there has been a steady dismantling of the physical enclosure in communities everywhere, partly because sisters have left their orders or moved into their own apartments. But also because the modern world has so thoroughly en-croached on this medieval way of life, pushing the nuns out of their natural habitats much like the deer and bears that wander into backyards when forests are razed for roadways and housing. A Benedictine community in Boulder, Colorado, closed down its abbey a few years ago because of the relentless expansion of nearby suburbia. As a neighbor told the *New York Times*, "Up until a few years ago, when you turned off the main road and entered the abbey, it was like you were in a different world. Now it's just too noisy to hear the prayers." (Occasionally, however, smoking sisters out of hiding isn't such a bad thing. In 1994 an ill-fated Idaho proposition that would strip homosexuals of basic protections prompted sisters from the century-old Monastery of St. Gertrude to make a public statement for the first time in their history, so incensed were they by this blatant affront to human rights.)

In 1997 a community of Carmelite nuns in Brooklyn decided to close its monastery after ninety uninterrupted years of its sacred routine. The vocations had dropped, and the hectic, embattled surrounding neighborhood was no longer conducive to peaceful prayer. Sad as the closing of the monastery was, the mother superior had to wonder if there wasn't another, better way—one more compatible with these times. Maybe a protected edifice wasn't necessary after all. "I really believe that perhaps one can return to the world and have your own place in secret," she told the *New York Times.* "There you can pray to the Father, who in secret can hear you."

As the monastery door locks, another, very different kind of convent opens, with new wings and extensions being added on every day. It is the convent of cyberspace, where thousands of women in chat rooms and news groups e-mail one another, sharing memories of pre–Vatican II life, venting about the latest ruling from Rome, sending cyber-farewells before entering the novitiate—communicating widely in time-honored silence, save for the clacking of the keys. Some send out prayer requests: "Please pray for a young woman in my parish who just found out she has breast cancer"; "I ask your prayers for my nephew who just lost his job." During the spring, subscribers to one such list received this e-mailed invitation: "You are welcome to share Lent in cyberspace at http://www.christworld.com." A rather impersonal notice for this most soulful of occasions. Still, thousands of worshippers were reached with the stroke of a key, and that is something.

The phenomenon of nuns in cyberspace is a real triumph, given how marginalized and effectively silenced they have been over the years—never invited to meetings or consulted on policy issues that affected their lives. Before Vatican II, orders had few real avenues of communication with one another, which in some cases prompted a divisive competitiveness and suspicion. But now they can reach out on the Internet, disseminate news, organize protests, and collect signatures—for instance, when a sister is dismissed from a teaching position in a seminary for imparting opinions that deviate from the Vatican party line.

And yet, is it possible that computer screens will become the new choirs and altars? Already there are websites that offer religious services and prayer circles of a sort. When actual bodies no longer come together and pool the physical energy of communal prayer, even in communities of two and three, isn't something essential lost forever? No matter how much society is revolutionized by the Internet, certain professions will always require a physical presence and a human touch. Surgeon and nurse are clearly among them. Maybe sister is, too.

The nuns' ranks have become so depleted that missionary work is increasingly being performed by laypeople, some of whom bring spouses and children with them overseas to nurse or teach for a period of years. Lay associates or co-members are also a growing phenomenon; they are laypeople who do not take vows but make a renewable commitment of usually one or two years and are welcome to participate in certain aspects of community life. Also gaining strength is the concept of lay ministry, wherein lay Catholics have the opportunity to play a role in church rituals, as well as provide counseling and religious education.

All that sounds reasonable—the church is for the people, and getting people more involved seems like a healthy idea. Yet some nuns feel threatened by the influx of the laity in the form of co-members into a world that has long been structured by strict vows and an undeniable exclusivity. Why allow people to enjoy the fruits of the life without having to endure the sacrifices? "We have several that come here," says a Loretto sister in her eighties. "Sometimes they just come to visit, or for a meeting, or to listen to some talks, or for Mass. Sometimes they spend a few days and relax. And my question to them is, 'What do you want? *What do you want.* Why are you doing this?' I don't seem to get a good answer. But it's something that is happening, and if I fought it, I'd be the loser." Of course, it wouldn't be the first time that the progressive Loretto sisters wrestled with a profoundly divisive issue. In 1980, when their chapel was being renovated, some traditionalists resisted the decision to replace the stained glass with clear windows that actually open—a vivid symbol of the Vatican II push for a greater interplay between the church and the world, and the Loretto commitment to social justice. That is, to a vision of religious life that extended well beyond themselves.

As for lay ministry, the Vatican seems leery. In 1997 Pope John Paul II approved a document that imposed several limitations on lay participation, among them: laypeople may not deliver homilies, hold the title "coordinator" or "chaplain," wear stoles or other liturgical garb, receive training in seminaries, or govern parishes. Clearly the Vatican wants to protect the rarefied realm of the clergy. But at the rate vocations are going, soon there might not be anyone left to deliver the homilies.

Compared with the number of priests, nuns' ranks are positively flush, outnumbering them almost two to one—yet another reason excluding women from the decision-making seems patently unjust. There simply are not enough priests to meet the need; many have to spread themselves thinly over many parishes. Still, the Vatican is unyielding in its position that women can't be ordained, adhering in part to a 1976 decree that claimed priests had to bear a natural resemblance to Christ. "The 'Penis Statement,' as we came to call it," Dominican sister Donna Quinn says, laughing. As Sister Joan McVeigh puts it, in a mock confrontation, "Many of our sisters have more theology than you. Is it because you have that little dangling thing that you can stand in front of me and preach?"

Donna Quinn, an iconoclast and a feminist, is the sort of sister who seems most alive while squaring off in a controversy; confronting bishops and cardinals has proved as exhilarating as it is scary. She held banners and sang protest songs with other nuns outside the Vatican when there was a synod taking place inside in which nuns had no voice. She has been an outspoken proponent of women's reproductive rights and women's ordination. And she was one of twenty-four publicly identified sisters who signed the 1984 ad in the *New York Times* that called for a dialogue on the issue of abortion. It was a step no sister took lightly.

The action prompted a swift and stern response from the Vatican. Cardinal Jean Jerome Hamer— "We called him 'Hammer,' " says Sister Donna—instructed the heads of religious orders to demand retractions from any members who had signed the ad.

Those who refused were to be threatened with dismissal. And while the two brothers and two priests who signed ultimately withdrew their statements, the nuns held out. A vituperative back-and-forth between various church factions, including Vatican representatives and canon lawyers, followed.

Several months later Cardinal Hamer came to Chicago to speak at the Holy Name Cathedral. Sister Donna saw an opportunity: Perhaps if she just talked to the cardinal about victims of rape and incest, who make the issue of abortion such a complex one, he would soften his position. So Sister Donna attended the sermon, wearing a black armband, symbolizing the death of the institutional church. Like-minded protesters marched outside, some of whom carried signs that said WE WANT A CHURCH FOR OUR DAUGHTERS.

At the end of his sermon the large, elegantly robed cardinal greeted a long line of well-wishers that included Sister Donna. When she reached him, she introduced herself.

"Suddenly he changed," Sister Donna says. "I could feel the evil. He looked down on me and said, 'You! You organized this whole protest! Who do you think you are?' So I stood there and said, 'I am a Dominican like you are, and I'm asking you, What would Dominic do at this time? If you want to be a good Dominican, you change your attitude and you retract that statement you made. I'm asking you to meet with the signers in person.' " But the Cardinal thundered, "I'll show you! You come to Rome! *I'll* give you a meeting."

"Now, I am not this brave," Sister Donna says. "I'm seeing dots in front of my eyes, the oxygen is going; I could not believe his response. I wanted him to know that there was a face and a body attached to these women that he felt like throwing out of their religious communities. But then I felt like I was going to faint, and I really didn't want the other women to see me fall down." Just then the supremely reasonable Cardinal Joseph Bernardin of Chicago, who happened to be nearby, grabbed hold of Sister Donna and said, "Sit here in front and don't pay attention to him."

Eventually some small compromise was reached. Cardinal Hamer pulled back on his threats in exchange for certain clarifications from the nuns, whose communities issued some ambiguously worded statements that went a long way toward appeasing the Vatican. Still, for a lot of nuns, the scars from that incident won't ever heal. To be threatened with expulsion simply for listening to your heart—the thought of it constituted a grievous betrayal.

"They've become so enamored of themselves," Sister Margaret Traxler says of the male hierarchy, her grandmotherly mien darkening with disgust. "They put on their scarlet robes and their ermine collars and their watered silk, and they just think they're the finest of the bird kingdom. But they are also the pigeons and vultures." As for the pope, Sister Margaret says, "He's keeping nuns down with his foot on the backs of our necks."

Here again is where outsiders find themselves at a loss. If nuns differ so fundamentally from the Vatican party line, why be a nun at all? What business does a freethinking feminist like Donna Quinn have being a nun anyway? When she is asked this, Sister Donna is momentarily transfixed by the irrelevance of the question.

"I'm a woman, a feminist, Irish, Catholic, a Democrat, a South-sider," she says finally. "These are the things you are. And I'm saying that the church I want for our daughters, the church I belong to, *I* own it. It's mine. Not yours"—meaning the pope and his retinue of Cardinal Hamers. "You are immoral, you are taking us down the wrong path."

Which is to say, the church is something bigger than the men who happen to be in power at any given time. As Sister Joan McVeigh describes it, "While I resented the hierarchy, I guess I came to think that that isn't the real church anyway. The real church exists in coming home after a fourteen-hour day, dragging your feet, coming in with a smile, and saying to a sister, 'Did you save me anything for supper?' That's the real church. The real church is helping the recovering alcoholic who had a slip. That's the real church. The real church is when you sneak some food out the back door of the convent for some man standing there, who's on the run. You ask no questions. That's the real church."

And the real nun? Being a nun is something deeper than living as an obedient charge of the Vatican. The identity isn't easily shed.

"It's what I am," says Sister Donna. "It's in my bones."

Institutional death can be as sad as the loss of a human life. As it atrophies and everyone starts to file out, the institution stands as a skeletal reminder of ideals and a way of life that once seemed so essential.

American nuns aren't gone yet, but there is unmistakable evidence of an era coming to an end. Even among the women in this book, harsh realities bred startling change in the few short years since I met them. Recently the Trappistines sold their cows. While their upkeep had given form to the lay sisters' day, they had finally become too costly and difficult for the community's aged sisters to maintain. For the Poor Clares of Greenville, South Carolina, the tradition of a revolving cast of priests traveling to the monastery to say Mass has ended, as a result of the priest shortage. Now the sisters, whose lives had been shaped by a communal spirit of enclosure in a prayerful place, must break into smaller groups and leave home to attend Mass at nearby parishes. Not long ago Sister Diana's cloistered community sold its pre–Civil War letterpresses and drawersful of hand type to make way for modern computer equipment—a heartbreak for the sisters who ran the presses for decades. The Daughters of Charity in St. Louis recently sold their baronial provincial house to the University of Missouri. Now sisters live in groups of four, five, and six in houses scattered throughout the city. Few wear a veil anymore; the "habit" has become a white blouse and blue skirt. As for Sara Stranz, the Daughter of Charity whose faith in God helped her conquer drug addiction, she has decided to leave religious life. After seventeen years of commitment and service, she has grown disillusioned by the inexorable mainstreaming of the sisters—the middle-class comforts, the lack of a real habit, the individualistic vocations and pursuits that, to her mind, have greatly weakened the spirit of community. Now she is teaching school in Tampa, Florida.

Is religious life a hapless casualty of our times, bound for extinction, having outlived its usefulness? Or will the twenty-first-century sister discover a new purpose? And if so, what sort of woman is best suited to fulfill it? For instance, does the current influx of women in middle age, with full-blown careers and even children behind them, somehow corrupt the idea of what nuns are supposed to be, or will they reinvigorate the institution with their worldliness and perspective? For some sisters the discussion has been wrenching, for others invigorating—a rare opportunity to reimagine their own future. Perhaps it is simply that fiery burst before the sun sets, but American nuns have never been more passionate about who they are and what is at stake.

Given the galloping fin de siècle amorality that we are all still reeling from, a return to the cloister and strict monastic customs would probably be applauded and supported by the laity—in essence allowing us to self-flagellate vicariously. (In recent years only cloistered orders have managed to attract a healthy number of new vocations.) But there is also a case to be made for the inclusiveness of full-scale modernization—for lay clothes, apartment living, and a stripped-down, streamlined novitiate. Habits are dated, and enormous motherhouses are grossly inefficient, considering the paltry number of women they serve. I am looking at some old French doors in my bedroom as I write this. Installed in 1908, they are pretty as can be, but they are also warped and splintering; in the winter, cold air slices through the gaps. To replace them with the double-paned aluminum variety seems a travesty, but these charming old doors just don't work anymore.

For some nuns, guessing the fate of the institution is an unseemly exercise. The future, even their own, is not for them to decide. Such women have relaxed into the notion that what will be will be. If religious life is passé, let it devolve naturally.

For her part, Sister Martha Ann Kirk has enduring faith in the cyclical nature of things. "My studies have made it so easy to see that in every century there have been emerging patterns of religious life. And sometimes because of political or economic realities, or because of different emphases in spirituality, these forms have died out," she says, sitting cross-legged in a sunny room on the second floor of her house, the day after Easter. "But somehow or another the spirit prevails. So I am sad that our particular group in the United States has an average age of seventy-two. I am fifty-three, and I'm planning on living at least thirty more years, and in thirty years will I be among the last Incarnate Word sisters in the United States? Perhaps.

"But we are in the Easter season now, and we need to trust in this process of death and resurrection and know that the God who always was and who always will be has a larger vision and bigger plans. And if people aren't practicing and naming themselves just the way we practice and name ourselves, that doesn't mean that this graced reality of people being called to deep prayer and generous service won't continue." Sister Margaret Traxler agrees. "Why are we so concerned that there be sisters? So that they can maintain our motherhouses and watch our cemeteries? Ha! The work of God will go on. There will always be dedicated women."

One hopes so. Now more than ever, our commercially driven society could benefit from the example of this inviolable sector so untainted by capitalism's oracular precepts. Even though nuns are sweating issues of productivity and solvency as much as anyone else, it is not financial pressure that will be their undoing. It is the soul-defeating business of attempting to gain ground within a system that systematically shuts them out—not allowing them (or any Catholic women) to answer a call to the priesthood, threatening to excommunicate conscience-driven dissenters on reproductive rights, commanding nuns and priests to quit ministering to homosexual Catholics, not taking nuns seriously. Given Pope John Paul II's righteous adherence to tradition, the Vatican has even encouraged a return to the habit and the strict, cloistered life, thereby attempting to reverse a metamorphosis that began nearly forty years ago. For the time being, many nuns are making do, having achieved a separate peace, their notion of church circumscribed by the street, the shelter, the people they meet. "Maybe Pope John Paul will be replaced by a John XXIII, or maybe he won't," says Sister Margaret. "To tell you the truth, it doesn't make any difference to me anymore. The men of the church think their job is to run a corporation without a deficit. But they don't run my life."

Yet the controversies continue, and for good reason. At the very least it seems only right and just that the institutional church accept women into the ranks of the clergy, thus ensuring them full participation in the faith to which they have devoted themselves utterly. The rationales against it—from the notion that priests must bear a physical likeness to Christ to the fact that Christ chose only men to be His Apostles—seem specious. As it is often said, by that thinking all priests would have to be bearded like Christ, as well as be Jews like both Christ and the Apostles. Furthermore, Christ's charging women with the rather monumental task of spreading the news of His resurrection could easily be interpreted as a call to ministry. But the Catholic Church is not a democratic institution, and there is a limit to how much it has to explain itself or make sense. For progressives, choosing to live under the aegis of such a system is to live every day with a considerable degree of frustration.

Maybe it seems silly for outsiders to be worried about the fate of Catholic nuns, but their presence has an impact on all of us. We are devastated when a stranger opens fire in a schoolyard. By the same token, a stranger's capacity for extravagant charity and sacrifice can be a revelation. The striving, self-satisfied CEO cannot help but pause upon reading about or seeing the good works of a nun, whose beneficence extends beyond Catholics. I had count-less prayers said for me during the course of this project, and they transformed me every time. For me, whether God existed or not was sort of beside the point in the moment that some wise old face was peering into mine with something akin to love. Even if nuns never crossed our paths, their vanishing would have a tragic element. Be it an obscure species in the rain forest or an order of nuns, extinction is like a miscarriage on a cosmic level— a link dropping out of the chain.

In mob movies the gun-wielding toughs always display an absurdly abashed sanctimony in the face of the clergy. With nuns they are protective—they put them on pedestals. It is as if these characters who wallow in vice need to know that at least some small corner of civilization is incorruptible. It balances them and allows them to be as damaged as they are.

It is a bit like that for the rest of us, too. Self-absorbed as we tend to be in the secular world, we are well acquainted with our flaws. So it is edifying to know that somewhere there are people who aren't as weak, self-centered, and acquisitive as we are. Somewhere there are people who have no price, who can with-stand the moral scrutiny that their station invites, in a way that so many in the all-male clergy cannot. Surely that is why we worry about what looks like the gradual secularization of nuns. The more their lives resemble ours, the more likely it seems that they will take on our failings. In a culture whose soul is shaped by profiteering media, someone has got to stand for something. We are so hungry for heroes.

There is heroism in the nuns who weathered Vatican II. Dur-ing a time when women were not supposed to be bold, they heeded their hearts and gave up everything for the love of God. The life was punishing; there was only trust and faith—mad love, as it is often called—to see them through. Of course, things didn't turn out as expected, but still the nuns honor their commitment, beating back the doubts that roll in regularly to this day.

A lot of those women have died. Many of the remaining ones are on their own now, worlds away from the crucible of the novitiate that made them. Women like Sister Joan McVeigh, who moved to a high-rise several years ago, where some of her sisters were already living. For a while they were a family—a real post–Vatican II community of religious women, going to Mass together, cooking together, eating together, sharing their struggles. "It was great," says Sister Joan. "Lovely. But one by one they went away. One retired, one got a high-track job in another place. . . . I'm the only one left.

"I live on the twenty-second floor. I can see the sun rise," Sister Joan says, squinting warmly at the thought, in that way of nuns who can be so thankful for so little. "The other day I turned around and there were a thousand monarch butterflies flying by. That's an exaggeration, perhaps, but not by much—they filled the window.

"Then they did kind of a loop-de-loop, like, 'So long!' " She illustrates with a jaunty wave. "And when I jumped up, they were gone."

SELECTED BIBLIOGRAPHY

Armstrong, Karen. *Through the Narrow Gate*. New York: St. Martin's Press, 1981.

Bernstein, Marcelle. *The Nuns*. Philadelphia: J. B. Lippincott, 1976.

Carey, Ann. *Sisters in Crisis: The Tragic Unraveling of Women's Religious Communities*. Huntington, Ind.: Our Sunday Visitor, 1997.

Curb, Rosemary and Nancy Manahan, eds. *Lesbian Nuns: Breaking Silence*. Tallahassee, Fla.: Naiad Press, 1985.

Ebaugh, Helen Rose Fuchs. *Women in the Vanishing Cloister*. New Brunswick, N.J.: Rutgers University Press, 1993.

Elm, Susanna. *'Virgins of God': The Making of Asceticism in Late Antiquity*. Oxford: Clarendon Press, 1994.

Gillis, Chester. *Roman Catholicism in America*. New York: Columbia University Press, 1999.

Godden, Rumer. *In This House of Brede*. London: Macmillan, 1969; reprint, New York: Fawcett, 1970.

Gramick, Jeannine, ed. *Homosexuality in the Priesthood and the Religious Life*. New York: Crossroad Publishing, 1989.

Griffin, Sister Mary. *The Courage to Choose: An American Nun's Story*. Boston: Little, Brown, 1975.

Harrison, V V. *Changing Habits: A Memoir of the Society of the Sacred Heart*. New York: Doubleday, 1988.

Hollingsworth, Gerelyn. *Ex-Nuns: Women Who Have Left the Convent*. Jefferson, N.C.: McFarland & Co., 1985.

Lieblich, Julia. *Sisters: Lives of Devotion and Defiance*. New York: Ballantine Books, 1992.

McCarthy, Mary. *Memories of a Catholic Girlhood*. New York: Harcourt Brace, 1957; reprint, San Diego: Harcourt Brace, 1985.

McEnroy, Carmel E. *Guests in Their Own House: The Women of Vatican II*. New York: Crossroad Publishing, 1996.

McNamara, Jo Ann. *Sisters in Arms: Catholic Nuns Through Two Millennia*. Cambridge, Mass.: Harvard University Press, 1996.

Medwick, Cathleen. *Teresa of Avila: The Progress of a Soul*. New York: Alfred A. Knopf, 1999.

Merton, Thomas. *The Silent Life*. New York: Farrar Straus Cudahy, 1956.

Norris, Kathleen. *The Cloister Walk*. New York: Riverhead Books, 1996.

Quinonez, Lora Ann, CDP, and Mary Daniel Turner, SNDdeN. *The Transformation of American Catholic Sisters*. Philadelphia: Temple University Press, 1992.

Rogers, Carole Garibaldi. *Poverty, Chastity, and Change: Lives of Contemporary American Nuns*. New York: Twayne Publishers, 1996.

Simpson, James B., ed. *Veil and Cowl: Writings from the World of Monks and Nuns*. Chicago: Ivan R. Dee, 1994.

Sisters, Servants of the Immaculate Heart of Mary, Monroe, Michigan. *Building Sisterhood*. Syracuse, N.Y.: Syracuse University Press, 1997.

Spink, Kathryn. *The Call of the Desert: A Biography of Little Sister Magdeleine of Jesus.* London: Darton, Longman and Todd, 1993.

Turk, Midge. *The Buried Life: A Nun's Journey.* New York: World Publishers, 1971.

Ware, Ann Patrick, ed. *Midwives of the Future: American Sisters Tell Their Story.* Kansas City, Mo.: Leaven Press, 1985.

Whitney, Catherine. *The Calling: A Year in the Life of an Order of Nuns.* New York: Crown Publishers, 1998.

Wong, Mary Gilligan. *Nun: A Memoir.* New York: Harcourt Brace Jovanovich, 1983.

ARTICLES

Gonzalez, David. "At Monastery in Brooklyn, an Era Ends." *New York Times*, 16 April 1997.

Louis, Meera. "Modern Marketing Helps Sell Life as a Nun." *Wall Street Journal*, 11 May 1999.

Sella, Marshall. " 'You Have a Cold Heart, Degas!' " (profile of Sister Wendy Beckett). *New York Times Magazine*, 26 January 1977.

———. "World Comes Too Close, Closing Down Old Abbey." *New York Times*, 29 June 1997.